POETRY COMPETITION
FOR 11-18 YEAR-OLDS

YoungWriters

POP!
The Power Of Poetry

Devon & Cornwall
Edited by Annabel Cook

 Young**Writers**

First published in Great Britain in 2006 by:
Young Writers
Remus House
Coltsfoot Drive
Peterborough
PE2 9JX
Telephone: 01733 890066
Website: www.youngwriters.co.uk

SB ISBN 1 84602 389 0

Foreword

This year, the Young Writers' *POP! - The Power Of Poetry* competition proudly presents a showcase of the best poetic talent selected from thousands of up-and-coming writers nationwide.

Young Writers was established in 1991 to promote the reading and writing of poetry within schools and to the young of today. Our books nurture and inspire confidence in the ability of young writers and provide a snapshot of poems written in schools and at home by budding poets of the future.

The thought, effort, imagination and hard work put into each poem impressed us all and the task of selecting poems was a difficult but nevertheless enjoyable experience.

We hope you are as pleased as we are with the final selection and that you and your family continue to be entertained with *POP! Devon & Cornwall* for many years to come.

Contents

Lydia Singer (12)	67
Holly Rampling (13)	68
Chloe MacGillivray (12)	69
Jenny Eveleigh (13)	70
Tom Marsden (12)	71
Sarah Wickes (12)	72
James Guilfoyle (13)	73
Dan Rogerson (12)	74
Emma Corrick (13)	75
Ashleigh Clayton (13)	76
Sam Petty (13)	77
Alastair Quinton-Tulloch (12)	78
George Snell (13)	79
Tom Young (13)	80
Victoria Charles (13)	81
Christie Woodley (13)	82
Joshua Braddick (13)	83

Hele's School, Plymouth

Elizabeth Tobin (12)	84
Katy Sheldon (13)	85
Jessica McGlinchey (12)	86
Shaun Curtis (12)	87
Luke Ambrose (12)	88
Kathryn Higgins (12)	89
Keesha Carter-McDonald (12)	90
Danielle Barnes (13)	91
Jade Ellery (12)	92
Douglas Miller (13)	93
Adam Stead (12)	94
Abigail Jones (12)	95
Laura Shepherd (12)	96
James Watson (12)	97
Lewis Kitte (12)	98
James Lee (12)	99

Lipson Community College, Plymouth

Holly Wilson (12)	100
Lucy White (12)	101
Siobhan Tracey (12)	102
Josh Steels (12)	103

Jessica Patrick (12)   104
Chanelle Newcombe (12)   105
Ella Kenny (12)   106
Stacey Hancock (12)   107
Hannah Baugh (12)   108
Lewis Barnes (12)   109

Liskeard School, Liskeard
Zachary Leon (13)   110

Plymouth Hospital School, Plymouth
Tim Sloman (15)   111
Kirsty Griffin (13)   112
Naomi Jones (17)   113
Aimee Clark (15)   114

St James' School, Exeter
Ashley Wonnacott (11)   115
Amber Goff (11)   116
Laura Tippett (12)   117
Charlotte Abdoviszadeh (12)   118
Luke Batchelor (11)   119
Abby Thomas (11)   120
Ben Burton (11)   121
Farihah Choudhury (11)   122
Ashley Hobbs (14)   123
Adam Rose (11)   124
Chelsea Lee (11)   125
Emma Jewell (11)   126
Ellen-Mary Haydon Wright (11)   127
Matthew Knight (11)   128
Matthew Channon (14)   129
Bethan Ashelford (11)   130
Kirsty Dare (14)   131
Simone Marillier (11)   132
Ummaymah Qureshi (11)   133
Sarah Wakeley (11)   134
Estelle Hacq (11)   135
Michaela Ward (11)   136

Alex Seabrook (12)   137
Mashud Rahman (11)   138

St Luke's Science and Sports College, Exeter
Sammy Cooper (11)   139
Daniel Kendall (11)   140
Hannah Aplin   141
Emily Hiscox (11)   142
Emma Rowett (11)   143
Kirsty Dean (13)   144
Zöe Rio (14)   145
Christopher Morris (13)   146
Dominic MacNamara (14)   147
Melissa Sampson (13)   148
Jade Willingham (13)   149
Katie Omand (11)   150
Steffanie Herd (11)   151
Charlotte Childs (14)   152
Ellie Sketchley (13)   153
Sally Foss (13)   154
Christopher Rand (13)   155
Max Bennett (13)   156
Matthew Ayton (14)   157
Becky Lee (13)   158
Sasha Lovell (13)   159
Sam Woodman (13)   160
Rachel Sharratt (11)   161
Bethany Meredith, Emily Ford & Megan Hobbs (11)   162
Faye Windsor (11)   163
Rieuan Elliott (11)   164

St Margaret's School, Exeter
Hannah Bolt (14)   165

Torquay Grammar School for Girls, Torquay
Emily Sheen (13)   166
Jen Huntington (12)   167
Millie Hawkins (12)   168
Alice James (12)   169
Caroline Hickey (11)   170

Trinity School, Teignmouth

The Poems

Stand Out From The Crowd

Do you see me closing down?
Shutting off from the outside,
I raise my hand to tell the answers,
But no one cares for it,
I see the glazed over eyes,
Through the haze of my own,
Head is spinning out of control,
Thumping like a grand steel band,
Cheeks become sore and tender,
A single tear falls,
Followed by a shower,
I am still,
Among a sea of creatures,
But no one seems to notice,
They point and sneer,
They say it's just attention,
I feel the pain,
Of wanting to care,
I want to feel,
For these are not flows of attention,
But of frustration,
Of not getting through this wall of ice,
Confusion collides with itself,
Inside my empty heart,
The hollowness I feel it,
I subtract inside myself,
I am lost,
To the world and myself,
I go to places: I don't want be.

Rachel Dickinson (15)

Seasons

Cool, calm and breezy,
Spring wakes me after winter's long sleep
The daffodils are emerging
As the lambs hop after the sheep.

        But here comes the sun's fiery roar,
        It's teasing my skin once again,
        It tickles, then burns,
        It stings and I yearn,
        For summer's pushed aside once again.

What's this I see?
The leaves are changing today
Red, orange and brown
And the once fierce sun, now weak in the sky,
Is slowly sinking away.

        And it's not long before winter's icy chill
        Leads me inside,
        Where fires are warm,
        Cold bodies lie still.

Sophie Thomsett (14)
Budehaven Community School, Bude

Seasons May Change; Winter To Spring But I'll Love You Until The End Of Time

In winter, I'll hold you with my thick white blanket of snow
Like the falling flurry of little snowflakes I'll be there for you,
I'll wrap you in my thick embrace
The toasty golden fingers of this season's fire will warm your heart
As will I whenever you're down because I will love you forever

In spring, we'll grow and new relationships will bud
Like flowers we'll flourish and prosper in the new-found sun
As the ice melts away our worries; our hearts will be filled with hope
I will tell the birds to sing your praises because I will love you forever

In summer, I'll kiss you with my sunny golden lips
Like the moving hills of water I'll refresh you
                              and wash out your troubles
As you surf down the face of summer's swell,
I'll be there in case you fall
I will pray for the sun to shine in both our hearts
Because I will love you forever.

In autumn, the leaves will fall and die but my love for you
                              will grow on strong
Like the fireworks brighten the sky,
You are the only thing that brightens my heart
As your sparkler fades in your gloved hand,
Your disappointed face looks at me;
You know I'll give you mine, just to see your smile
Because I will love you forever.

Alys Collins (14)
Budehaven Community School, Bude

Season

The beginning of a new year,
As the snow starts to melt,
Sights of brown dead leaves come to view,
Crisp of the leaves as I stomp and stamp,
Leaves crumble in my hands.
Winter transfers to spring,
Offspring of animals jump and leap,
Flowers reach out towards the sun,
As it blankets the sky.
Soon enough spring ends,

But soon enough it starts to rain,
As autumn comes to view,
Trees start to go brown and die,
And leaves start to crisp.
At the end of the year,
Icicles glisten, snow covers the ground,
And stockings hang above the fireplace,
Christmas is here again,
But now it has ended
The end of another year.

Teagen Hill (14)
Budehaven Community School, Bude

Seasons May Chance

Spring jumps to summer, hoping for a sun-kissed smile.
Creatures arise,
Will only last for a while.

Summer turns to autumn,
Trees are a crimson shade,
The colourfulness of the world is surely soon to fade.

As autumn turns to winter smiles are lost,
Windowpanes are smothered, the rooftops' layer of frost.
A chill creeps up on you like a ninja in the night,
We are hoping this will return next year
This wonderful glacial sight.

Winter then returns to spring,
The horizon starts to melt,
The change between the seasons is surely to be felt.

Andrea Hughes (15)
Budehaven Community School, Bude

Season Smiles

Spring promises resolutions and new beginnings,
Lambs in fields dance playfully,
Daffodils brighten hedgerows around,
Easter eggs piled high, ready to be eaten.

Summer brings smiles, suncream and snorkelling,
Waves crash, shattering like glass,
Ice cream drips on tiny hands and faces.
School is forgotten, for now anyway.

Autumn shimmers green and red,
Uniform is worn, hair neat, hands clean,
Blackberries fill pies made proudly by Granny,
Witches and ghosts bring fun to October.

Winter sparkles like diamonds and pearls,
Snow falls slowly, gracefully on bare branches,
Trees stand tall, draped in tinsel and baubles.
Children wait patiently for sleigh bells and Santa.

Natasha Slee (14)
Budehaven Community School, Bude

Those Perfect Summer Days

I wake to the soft heat of the sun
Burning my face,
Groggily I open my eyes
Heavy from the long late summer nights,
I glance over to the corner of my room
Notice my board,
My eyes peacefully shut again as I remember
Those perfect, glassy sets the evening before.
I know soon I will hear the soft tick over
Of that familiar old white van,
The smell of diesel will fill my nose,
The door will slam
My name will be yelled.
My wetsuit hangs on my board,
Ready, waiting for me,
My heart races as I think about getting back out there,
Sitting, waiting, wishing
For that next beautiful wave.
The glistening blue ocean surrounding me
Laps against my thighs,
Beads of salt water run down my forehead
And drip from my hair.
I feel as if I don't have a worry in the world.
That is why I love so much,
Those perfect summer days.

Lucy Barnes (14)
Budehaven Community School, Bude

Somewhere Over The Rainbow

The rainbow is a colourful, mysterious and mystical rare existence;
It only comes out when there is a mixture of sunshine and rain.
Where does the rainbow end?
Who knows?
Is there a meaning for the colours of the rainbow?
Who knows?
To be honest I don't want to know;
I'd rather it stay a secret
I'd rather not know
Are the colours there
Or are they just a figment of our imaginations?
All the colours, all the wonders
Some things are better left unknown!

Danielle Naish (13)
Budehaven Community School, Bude

Teens' Years

Spots and fashion, heels a must
Boys and make-up, a bigger bust!
Healthy eating, homework and friends
Mum and Dad driving me round the bend.
A life as a teen isn't much fun
Sometimes I want to shout, 'Give me a gun!'
Instead pass my lippy
My hair needs a brush
Mousse, gel and hairspray really is a must
And can't forget music
Volume 10 is a blast
Remember moisturiser
I'm getting old fast.
Now it's time to sleep
It's the end of the day
Night Mum, night Dad,
Move over teddy, you're in the way!

Jessica Fewkes (12)
Camborne Science & Community College, Camborne

About Teenagers

Here I am, a teenager,
It doesn't feel like me,
My body keeps on changing,
I want to be set free.

Here I am a teenager,
Starting puberty,
Growing lots of body hair,
All over me.

Here I am a teenager,
Spotty as can be,
My face is getting spottier,
Please help me.

Here I am a teenager,
Getting into everything,
Like mobile phones and money,
And also smoking.

Here I am, a teenager,
Going to lots of parties with a hex,
Drinking booze and having sex,
With my ugly ex.

At least I am finishing my teens now,
Happy as I can be,
Now I am starting my twenties,
How bad can it be?

Liam Smith (12)
Camborne Science & Community College, Camborne

I Am A Teenager

Nobody knows my stress.
It's like an electronic press.
Nobody knows what it's like to be me.
Sometimes I wish they'd set me free.

Nobody wants me
This is how it's meant to be.
Sometimes I wish they'd set me free.
But this is how it's meant to be.
I wish they'd set me free.
Nobody knows what it's like to be me.

Thomas Fry (12)
Camborne Science & Community College, Camborne

Teenage Years

Nobody wants to know me anymore,
Now my voice has changed.
Getting stressed and slamming the door,
Me and my family are estranged.

All the time I'm getting stressed,
Getting thrown out of the house.
I've got to learn to relax and rest,
Then I feel bad, and feel like a little mouse.

Nobody knows what it is like to be me,
All the spots on my face.
I just wish they would let me be,
The girls think I'm a disgrace.

But I'll have to face it, get on with my life,
Forget the spots and get on with school.
I'll just remember they're the ones that look the fool,
And that is my teenage life.

Sam Frape (13)
Camborne Science & Community College, Camborne

Seashore

S unbathers slumbering on the shimmering sand.
E ager children catching crabs.
A bove the clouds seagulls cry.
S inging seals go swimming by.
H elpless surfers go.
O ver the waves.
R ed rays of sun.
E nds each day.

Jack Lipscombe (12)
Camborne Science & Community College, Camborne

Gargoyles

Gargoyles are cool when they fly
When I see them in a shop I just need to buy
Goblins are good but sometimes they're green
So I paint them like rock so they look mean.

Dragons are my favourite, they are cool
I want them to drag down a big, big wall
I collect them all, I always buy
I want to see a phoenix fly.

Aaron Kempe (12)
Camborne Science & Community College, Camborne

Teenagers

Thoughts are running through my head
Wondering what to do,
Wishing I was dead
Feelings that I'm going through.

It's hard to understand,
The emotions that I feel,
I need a guiding hand
To let me know what is real.

My friends are hard to work out
When we argue and fight,
They sometimes suss me out without a doubt
And I can see a red light.

All I want to do is go home
And lie peacefully on my own,
I feel like I'm a big dome
And cramped like an ice cream cone.

I am starting to feel pain
As my body is growing,
My temper is like a train
And my face is red and glowing.

My stomach is groaning
It's like I'm hungry but I'm not,
And I'm always moaning
As well as very hot.

I feel like I'm in love
With a very special lad,
I can fly away like a dove
Before my dad gets mad

At the end I am a teenager
Life has lessons for me to learn.

Josie Trescowthick (12)
Camborne Science & Community College, Camborne

Here I Am, A Teenager

Here I am a teenager
I am getting older
My teenage years are almost over
Now I am getting older

Here I am a teenager
My years are coming to an end
There were ups and downs
But I'm glad it has come to an end.

Dean Warren (12)
Camborne Science & Community College, Camborne

One Truth

I wake up,
Darkness forbids,
I get up,
A glint of red
Surpasses my honest eyes,
The source lies on my palms,
Waiting in haunted silence,
My head follows the trace to find my hand
Burning red with the truth,
That I as a child had never liked,
A sliver,
Just a sliver of blood
Falls from my skin.

Not mine;
His.
He's gone,
He's gone,
Perhaps to a worse place,
Perhaps not.

Sara Nicholas (12)
Camborne Science & Community College, Camborne

My Imaginary World

My imaginary world is above the clouds,
The houses are gingerbread and candy,
The sky is pink, orange and yellow like the sunset,
Everyone is flying.

The tree stumps are made of pure silver,
The branches are made of chunks of gold,
The sun is a giant pink ball of fluff,
The grass sprouts money flowers every hour.

I look around, something flew above me,
It was a unicorn with wings as white as snow,
I approached it and touched it with the tip of my finger,
It was soft, the horn was as stiff as a sword in a stone.

In my imaginary world,
The air is clean and fresh,
There's no pollution or storms,
The sea is free of sewage and long slimy seaweed.

Everyone has their own pot of wishing dust,
To have a happy life,
In my imaginary world,
You can talk and understand animals.

My house is the biggest of them all,
My room could fit 10 jeeps in it,
It has a four-poster bed with cream drapes,
When you walked through the double doors
Your feet sunk into the furry carpet.

There was a wooden dressing table with lots of accessories,
The crystal chandelier sparkled when the sun shone onto it,
And my pussycat lay sleeping,
On the puffy cushion which sat upon the chair.

In my imaginary world there is no war or fighting,
No murder,
Or violence,
No crime!

Ashleigh Mitchell (12)
Camborne Science & Community College, Camborne

Teenagers

T een years have arrived.
F very one of us all changing.
E motions all over the place.
N o one can tell me what to do.
A gony with spots and period pains.
G etting stressful by each passing day.
E ars being blasted by loud music.
R ules don't apply to me.
S moking and swearing - not for me.

Nicolle James (12)
Camborne Science & Community College, Camborne

My Future

My future is filled with wonderful things
No jellyfish or bumblebee stings
Pink trees and houses made of candy
I'll go to the beach and get all sandy.

Lots of people in the crowded streets
Children eating lots of treats
A chocolate factory for me and you
Take one bar or maybe two.

We could go to Florida for a holiday
Or instead we could go to Carbis Bay
A big mansion for a home
I brush my hair with a comb.

Sophie Phillips (12)
Camborne Science & Community College, Camborne

Being A Teenager Is Like . . .

Being a teenager is like . . .
You're fighting the world all the time,
Nobody's there and no one cares,
You can't speak instead like a mime,
But watch and stare as your dreams tear.

Being a teenager is . . .
Kinda rubbish though not all that bad,
People trust you more,
But memories fade that you once had,
Then your childhood closes like a door.

Rachael Penrose (12)
Camborne Science & Community College, Camborne

The Wave Rider

The surfer was happy riding over the waves,
He didn't know what was coming.
Happy and joyful with the red-hot sun beating over him.
The surfboard suddenly had a mind of its own.
The surfer was scared, scared of what would happen.
His crippled body lay by the sharp, pointy edges of the massive rock.
Covered in blood, alone and scared.
No one was there to help.

Jordon Stephens (12)
Camborne Science & Community College, Camborne

Horses, Horses

Horses, horses they're the best,
They are definitely better than the rest.

They run around in the wild,
Feeling like they are our child.

Their lovely shining eyes in the moonlight,
But they think it's just the food light.

Jumping over big fat poles,
But some of them are just too old.

Going out on a hack too,
Watch out they might do a poo!

Will trot back to the stables
And unpack the smelly hay bales.

I will come back tomorrow do some jumping,
Hope the horses won't be bucking!

Leanne Treloar (12)
Camborne Science & Community College, Camborne

Reaper

Look into my eyes and you will know I am the Reaper.
My rage and my anger boiling like seething.
I am the undertaker and I will take your soul
And bury you six feet deep into a big black hole.
I am turned on by broken bones and bloodshed.
You cannot kill me because I'm already dead.
I love that you are afraid, I love the stench of your fear.
When you hear the sound of funeral bells, you know that I am near.
Get into a fight with me, you'll never survive.
I'll stuff you in a body bag and bury you alive.
Lurking in the shadows, filling humans with fright.
My heart is colder than the Arctic, and darker
                              than a thousand midnights.
I am the Lord of Darkness, the epitome of evil.
You cannot defeat me, because your mind is weak and feeble.
I am draconic and sadistic to the bone.
I'll choke slam you and finish you off with the tombstone.
I will throw you into an inferno, and watch you burn.
They place your ashes into Paul's urn.
You cannot hide from me, I'm the real life boogie man.
When the lights go out, better run while you can.
Try to put an end to me, you'll have a date with my fist.
And when I get through you will wish you didn't even exist.
I am a merciless, ruthless beast.
And may your decaying, rotten carcass . . . *rest in peace!*

Kayleigh Webster (13)
Camborne Science & Community College, Camborne

He's Here!

I can see him,
In my dreams and all.

He's here,
He's here,
He's everywhere.

I can remember,
When he held me for the first time,
His hands are softer,
Than a kitten born just in time.

I lost him when I was five,
That day I touched a hive.

I miss him more and more,
I will see him one day
When I go through the door.

Up to Heaven
And never more.

Tamsyn Wills (12)
Camborne Science & Community College, Camborne

Forever In My Mind

Each day I lie,
On my bed in tears,
Wishing it wasn't true.

I never thought,
It would come to this,
Just because she had the flu.

I will cry forever -
Forever I will cry,
Why oh why did my nan die?

She will stay for eternity in my mind,
As she was gentle and incredibly kind.

Sarah Wright (12)
Camborne Science & Community College, Camborne

Food

Food is delicious, food is great
Food is one of my best mates.
Some foods are healthy and some are junk
But most of all it makes us plump.
Everyone needs food to make us grow
But most of all it makes us glow.

Some foods are horrible
Some foods are nice
But most of them are sumptuous and nice.
Foods are a special thing
Some are tasty, horrible and nice
Some are popular, especially curry and rice.

Kirsty Gilbert (13)
Camborne Science & Community College, Camborne

The Tabby Cat Of Albany

The tabby cat of Albany asks herself
Who is the stranger that enters our gate
All but every day,
Who is she?
Where is she from?
Why does she come here?
Why does she push that black and white print through my door?
Why does she stand on the rose petals
And brush her coat on the tulips?
Why is she out in the cold?
Who would want to be?
I would want to be curled up
With my master and mistress
Being petted and stroked
Watching every spark of the flame in the fire
Who is she?
Why is she here?
All but every day?

Joanne Rolling (12)
Camborne Science & Community College, Camborne

Baby May

The children run,
The children cry,
The fire is here
There's nowhere to hide
I open the door
There she lay
I check her pulse
1, 2, 3

She's alive! She's alive!
I grab her tight in my arms,
I run, I run
But then the wall collapses on me
Hiding me so no one can see
I have my baby sister only 10 weeks old
Holding her tightly, trying to act bold
But in this monument of distress
I have to confess
I am scared, I am scared
This is one hard test
I do not want to let her down

But then all goes black and I am back in my room
I run to my sister's bedroom
She's exactly where she's meant to be
It was all a dream
Why oh why did I dream
This awful scene?

Hannah McNamee (12)
Camborne Science & Community College, Camborne

The Detention Invention

Young Nathan from Camborne School
was caught whilst being a fool.
It's a terrible invention
this thing called detention,
you get it for breaking the rule.

Young Daniel from Camborne School
was caught whilst pinging some rubber,
whilst being told off he swore at Teacher
and was chewing on Hubba Bubba.

Young Jordan from Camborne School
was caught whilst kicking his brother,
the teacher phoned home and he was in trouble,
then in came his angry mother.

Nathan Barry (12)
Camborne Science & Community College, Camborne

Baggy Point In Croyde

The golden sun, bold and bright,
The blue sky lovely and light,
The sea relaxing and cold.
Waves smashing against Baggy,
In a peaceful, smooth way!
The breeze beautiful and gentle,
Whilst making waves of grass,
The sea drifting down with sea all around,
Orange and violet,
Totally silent.
The sun nearly gone . . . gone!
The sun rises with a beautiful colour,
A lovely orange yellow.
Then . . .
The sea angry and mad!
The sun lonely and sad,
Clouds storming across the sky,
I see this through my devil eye,
The sea shining and sparkling,
Like a mirror,
With reflections bouncing off it.
The sea quiet and calm,
Like a diamond charm.

This is my Baggy Point.

Eleanor Parker (11)
Edgehill College, Bideford

The Horrific Storm

The horrific lightning laughed as it smashed onto the school.
The torrential rain giggled as it drenched the school grounds.
The dictionary fell off the shelf as the heavy door smashed shut.
The sun was fighting to get through the clouds but was losing.
As the storm finished all was quiet in the school until . . .
The children returned!

Thomas Dimelow (11)
Edgehill College, Bideford

One Day

One day slavery will stop,
One day charges will drop.

One day poaching will be banned,
'As well as homework' hope the school gang.

One day recycling will reach the top,
Reusing, reproducing the whole lot.

One day parliament will know what children think,
And our thoughts will be put down in ink.

One day smoking will be a thing of the past,
As well as hunting that didn't last.

One day my beliefs will be put to the test,
And people will find they work best.

Laura-Mae Cunningham (11)
Edgehill College, Bideford

Coming Home

I was coming home from school one day,
When to my surprise,
Two green flying saucers,
Came flying from the skies.

The aliens picked me up at once,
Then to my dismay,
The aliens gave me sweeties,
And asked if I could play.

They whizzed me over Timbuktu,
And over gay Paris
Skimming the Atlantic Ocean,
And the deep blue sea.

They took me to their leader,
They took me to their king.
He was green and slimy,
His name was Keechowping.

They zapped me down to my street.
I was standing all alone,
When my mum asked where I'd been;
I said just coming home.

Cerys Erwood (12)
Edgehill College, Bideford

Homeless

I lie here in the cold wrapped up in a quilt,
Sitting in the doorway of a new shop that's been built.

I have no money, no food to eat,
I've walked a long way and have blisters on my feet.

I put out my cap for generous passers-by,
But the amount of money is never high.

I was thrown out of my home at the age of sixteen,
Troubled by the knowledge of what I'd seen.

Since then I've tried to manage and cope,
Things will get better! I pray and hope.

I hate my life, it's not my fault that I'm here.
All of the rich people think that it's queer.

Queer to be, and to look like me,
This is a day in the life of me.

Stephanie Green (12)
Edgehill College, Bideford

Dreams . . .

Splashing, thrashing,
Swimming in the sea,
That is where
I long to be.

Hanging, swinging,
Playing in the wood,
That is where I would be
If I could.

But here I am,
Stuck indoors,
Doing my homework,
Doing my chores.

How I long
To be outdoors,
To explore the country,
The hills and the moors.

To learn a new thing,
To see a new sight,
To wander about freely
All through the night.

To return at long last,
At the break of dawn,
To look out of my window
At the dewy lawn.

Nicola Grant (12)
Edgehill College, Bideford

The Beggar

Crawling around
On the rough, dirty street.
Pawing and patting
And begging at my feet.

Others turn away,
Muttering words of disgust,
Aimed at the beggar-boy,
Sitting in the dust.

Turning around
He singles me out,
Begging with his eyes,
Without uttering a shout.

I toss him a penny
And he runs away.
Off to tell his friends
What he's earned for today.

He's back in a minute,
With all his beggar friends.
They all want something,
So the begging never ends.

Joanne Grant (12)
Edgehill College, Bideford

The Panther

Silently it weaves
Like a fish in water,
Through the undergrowth
Searching for prey.

Black as night
Green eyes glistening
In the morning light,
Leading a lonely life.

Then prey has been sighted,
Springing forwards
The panther gives chase,
After the fleeing animal.

Through the jungle speeds the animal
But the panther, swifter than lightning
Is gaining ground,
Not giving up.

At last, hard work has paid off
The panther tucks in
To its well-earned feast
And drifts off into a well-earned rest.

Jack Cobb (12)
Edgehill College, Bideford

Fire

Flames dancing up the dusty chimney,
Flickering hot, orange sparks.
Dry logs giving the fire fuel,
And many colours reminding me of a hot sunny day.

Ashes piled up under the grate,
Crushed between the logs,
Dusty, thick and grey,
Then they blow swiftly away.

Heat from the fire warms a room,
Encourages doors to be opened.
It flames furiously, crackles, pops,
Then it dies down to ashes to be lit another day.

Jessica Berry (11)
Edgehill College, Bideford

The Classroom

It's 8.30am on Monday,
Everyone's coming to school,
The classroom's full of children,
All of them playing and acting the fool.

They're jumping about on the tables,
And writing things on the board,
They're sneaking around in each other's lockers,
And stealing things they can't afford.

They're shouting rude words out the window,
Acting without any cares,
But suddenly the teacher comes in,
And they all seat themselves on their chairs.

Now, this teacher is a very strict teacher,
Who doesn't like naughty kids,
And if something went wrong in *his* classroom,
He would burst into angry fits!

Everyone was dead silent,
As the teacher scanned the class,
All the children dropped their eyes to the floor,
And let the teacher's gaze pass.

The teacher examined the children closely,
And said, 'Now all find something smart to do.'
They all reluctantly, got out their school books.
I wouldn't like to be in that class, would you?

Rowan Styles (12)
Edgehill College, Bideford

My First Day At School

My first day at school was a horrible trip,
I pushed open the door, oops - slip!
I fell to the floor, flat on my face,
I was filled with horror and in disgrace!

They all giggled and laughed at me on the ground,
I was very late, I then found!
This was going to be a very long day,
But first it was maths, hip hip hooray! (Not)

'Um, excuse me,' I said to a girl,
'No talking in class Davis!' the teacher shouted at me.
'Detention right away!'
'Yes Madam,' I replied.

After spending three hours in the headmaster's office,
Sitting at an old, damp, dusty desk,
Writing 'I will never talk in class again' one million times
It was eventually time to leave!

Next was lunch, now that has to be better.
I signed in to the man at the desk, 'Mary-Lee Davis,' I said.
'Ah yes, I've heard all about you! Go on in,' he replied with a frown,
I ran to the queue and waited . . .

I clutched a knife and fork in my hand,
A lady then splattered some mushy peas on my plate!
'Eat it! she said with force,
I sat down at a table on my own, everyone stared at me.

After lunch I then went home,
I told my parents about the school,
And how I never got to play,
But then there's always another day!

Elizabeth Hanner (13)
Edgehill College, Bideford

The Coast

As the sand rubbed against my feet,
The ocean lapped along the shore
And began to warm over the heat
Of the bare coarse sand for evermore.

As I walked along the beach
And the sun was falling over the ocean,
Behind was left a trail of footsteps
That would only be washed away by the forbidding sea.

My journey would eventually finish,
But for now, the sun was gone,
And the sea was calm.
All that could be heard were the endless waves.

John Hodgson (13)
Edgehill College, Bideford

One Life!

When the dawn breaks, and the sun appears
The smell of day again, wipes away your tears
The darkness has passed by for another day,
This is home, and this is where you want to stay.

Don't live your life in sorrow, don't waste another day
This is your life, no one else's, live it your own way
Find something you love, and hold onto it tight
Never let it wander out of your sight.

This world won't live forever it will soon fade away and die,
And all those questions won't matter, you will just ask yourself why?
There will be no turning back, time cannot rewind,
Memories and regrets will be running through your mind.

When life gets tough, and you feel you want to die
And nothing seems to go right, no matter how hard you try.
I can't persuade you to stay, this is your life after all
But don't rely on me to catch you when you fall.

When the end comes, you won't feel any pain
The sun will disappear, and down will pour the rain.
The darkness unfolds, and you begin to feel numb
Knowing your life and all your memories are done!

Shonagh Dowdle (14)
Edgehill College, Bideford

Always There

Soaked though; silver, glistening drops of tears and rain,
Fresh memories of the cruel words spoken,
Through angry screams; your soul bruised, my heart broken.
I promise myself not to be hurt again.
Regret of the past driving me insane,
I saw two black eyes, then I was awoken
To the concern raining through each drip a love token;
With whiskers and tail, she recognised my pain.
So there we sat, I knew it was true,
A friend I never knew she'll always be.
She's always there, whether I'm sad or blue.
When all alone, she will sit by my side;
To know she's around is assuring to me.
When I have no one else; she'll see me through.

Roseanne Bromell (14)
Edgehill College, Bideford

Lingering Love

The cold, marble floor echoes her falling tears,
As, by the window, patiently she faces her fears.
She makes no sound. In sorrow, her heart is drowned,
In the dark, dead light, the walls and floor frown.
Will he ever return to her from the Great War,
Or will he die, as her cousin had before?

Mirrored glass reflects her desolate despair,
Her heart is stained, yet will he ever care?
The marble holds her as she sits in its palm,
Sadness it feels, yet it makes no alarm,
Such a soft beauty, with silk, brunette hair.
With one man only, her life, will she share.

The sky drizzled tears, whimpered with her grief.
Her almond, hazel eyes searched for belief.
She waited years, yet her love felt betrayed,
Discovering he was on another crusade.
Yet her hopes and dreams anchored to him alone,
But their cherished fulfilment was postponed.

Years passed by; his presence she never knew
The passion within her was never subdued
Silky silver threads now frame her withered mask,
His paper vision is clasped within her knotted grasp.
Her tide recedes leaving pebbles of resplendent gold.
Her spirit soars unlocked and uncontrolled.

His spirit relives past seasons and recalls
A waiting maiden, so young, so appalled
By the war that did isolation impose.
Yet her love is like a summer rose,
Whose sweet fragrance fills the air and
Pink petals outward fan, to embrace her handsome man.

Michelle Smith (14)
Edgehill College, Bideford

The Numbness

The numbness,
Pain fades, yet you know it's still there,
A dreamy nightmare,
Lined with a stained knife,
Please define reality,
Once I tried and failed.

For my contribution I gave you thought,
But it only thought,
Never acted,
Now the thought gradually drains.
I long for assistance,
Ease of pain no longer an ambition,
Just to live,
The simplicity of the greatest of wishes,
One more night,
Help me.

I plead in vain,
Lack of speed, I am slain,
You are burdened,
And I just another one,
In the falling procession,
Juggling precious lives,

An ambulance came to my house today,
Seconds too late.

I fell,
Imagination lives on?

Philip Watson (15)
Edgehill College, Bideford

Don't Rise Above Love!

If you'll give me a chance,
I'll put my arms around you -
Comfort you from this pain.

I'll sing to you,
When words are hard to find,
Or when it starts to rain.

When the tears collecting in your eyes,
Grow deep and start to fall,
I want you to know I'll always be here,
And I'll help you to stand tall.

If there's a problem you can't solve,
I'll help to decipher it.
Because we're all we need in life,
This bond of ours is fixed.

One day you'll see me, for who I am,
A caring soul in love.
You'll help me, as I have you,
When I taught you to *rise above!*

Miranda Gent (15)
Edgehill College, Bideford

Otters

I like otters, they are sweet,
I like otter's feet, they're neat,
I like otter's claws, well short claws,
Otter's claws upon their paws,
I like otters by the lake,
I'd give away my house for their sake,
I like otters, I hope they like me,
I wish I had an otter on my knee,
I like otters although they are wet,
I wish I had one for a pet!

Claudia Hardy (11)
Edgehill College, Bideford

The Sunset

When the summer's sun starts to set,
I rush to my window, eager to see
The brilliant colours fade slowly away,
An amazing and beautiful sight for me.

At first I noticed the clear blue sky,
So peaceful, pale and lovely too.
Not a cloud to be seen on this particular night,
There are not many days like this, only a few.

A striking red meets my eye,
A warm orange follows by,
A tranquil yellow is next in line,
Then maroon the colour of wine.

A luscious lilac, calm and light,
A relaxing and yet vibrant sight.
Next a coral which blends in well,
Then pastel pink, its tale to tell.

I watch the sky with anticipation
To see what colours come next,
But when they start to go away,
I feel so sad and perplexed.

The colours all blend into darkness,
And the sun goes down as a sign,
That the beautiful sight is now a dark night,
And I watch the shimmering stars shine.

Brisa Sanders-Hill (12)
Edgehill College, Bideford

Spring

Spring is the time of year,
Where evil leaves and peace re-appears,
The water flows from their ice-cold coffin,
And the early birds sing a peace pouring song.

Animals who sleep throughout the winter days,
Start the day, rolling in their nests of golden grey hay,
Sheep bounce out of their pens like creamy white clouds,
Whilst chickens cluck together like a fussy crowd.

Moles come out of their muddy grass burrow,
But still the sloths use the tree as a wooden brown pillow,
Lions who sleep in the springtime Savannah wakes
                                        up with mighty yawn,
When a small, alone mouse in a farm searches for corn.

So spring, spring an opening year,
Everything new, just like a babies first tear,
Flower that sprouts like a phoenix from the ashes,
In a garden riding from snowy marshes to a spring, green meadow.

Cameron Mitchell Banks (11)
Estover Community College, Estover

Red Shoes

She's dancing on her demons
There's fire in her feet
Flames panache fusion meet.
Her shoes scream stop,
Look at us,
We're alive,
Fugitives from normal drive.
She's stamping with a vengeance,
Power snaps her heels,
Girl with red shoes,
Is clinging to the wheel,
Voluptuous is her treading,
Deep luxury owns her stride,
On wings of bleeding passion ride.

Annie Ritson (13)
Great Torrington Community School, Torrington

Sydney House

Goodness me what a sight
7:35 out went the light
The fire grew with all its might
From the linen room that's right.

Goodness me, sigh
All the children gave out a cry.
Oh dear, oh my
Five little boys had to die.

Goodness me what a pain,
The house had seen.
Wounded soldiers shirt, bloodstain,
The Red Cross carrying so keen.

Goodness me, the house was grand
William built it in 1887
Made it with Malta and sand
William watched from Heaven.

The sadness it brought,
The fire it caught,
The people who fought,
William thought.

Bring it down without delay,
Don't leave it to decay,
Remember the little boys we may
Remember them every day.

Joshua Cooke (12)
Great Torrington Community School, Torrington

Mother Earth Hears Two Boys Crying

Mother Earth hears two boys crying,
One full of life, but the other is dying.

One wants a bike but his parents say no.
They say, 'Just use your old one, go on now go!'
He says, 'It's a rubbish one,'
His parents say, 'It's fine!'
He says, 'But everyone's got one that's better than mine!'
He throws a paddy, he goes upstairs,
He sits there sulking, 'It's just not fair!'
He says his parents are definitely the worst,
He's crying so much he just might burst!

The other boy's crying because he wants something to eat,
He needs some shoes on his cold, damp feet.
There's a puddle on the floor where his mother had cried
She'd sat there grieving for her son who'd died.
His father comes back with something to eat
A bone that is covered in hardly any meat.
What he has searched for he gives to his son
Who he needs to protect because he's the last one.

Mother Earth hears two boys crying,
One's full of life, but the other is dying.

Genna Ash (11)
Great Torrington Community School, Torrington

Sister's Are The Best!

Sisters are the best,
Although they're pests,
That's what they're for,
Arguing and fighting,
That's what they're for,
Good job they're here,
Else we will be bored.
Big sister's are cool,
They can be fools,
Boys are the best,
According to the rest.

Younger sisters are sweet,
They are the best to me,
Especially Fee,
Who is good to me.

Jess Slade (12)
Great Torrington Community School, Torrington

Give Love

I am writing this poem,
Because of the world we are living in.
There are break-ins and stealing
And nasty people who like killing.
People hurt other people just because of their religion.
But nobody cares and nobody listens,
Why can't the government do something about this?
Many people are poor, hungry and sick,
They die of starvation, but still there is no communication.
Many people are dying, many people are crying,
But no one is caring and no one is sharing.
How can we stop this and how can we care?
We could give money and food and we could all share.
Together we could stop this all,
We just need to stand tall,
Our greed is unmanageable our greed is selfish.
We could stop all this and help the people who need it.
When you're in bed and tucked in tight,
Think of those poor people out in the cold night,
Just a little bit of love is all we need to give,
Helping other people and the way they live,
We need to care for them, but my question is how?
This greed and obsession needs to stop right now!

Amy Cooper (11)
Great Torrington Community School, Torrington

A Place Of Tranquillity

The bustle, the flurry and fuss,
Melted away in a moment.
Through a door in her mind,
She entered that place full of hush.

The lake drifted around her
And a serene sunset sat shimmering behind hills.
Her eyes reflected its beauty,
Nothing wrong could possibly occur.

The air soothed her problems
And caressed her outer skin,
She detached herself from loneliness
And isolated herself from sin.

Her heart wrenched her away,
The next moment;
To the bustle, furry and fuss,
But she knows she belongs in that place,
Full of hush.

Jemimah Lane (14)
Great Torrington Community School, Torrington

May

Here we are in the month of May,
Wanting the sun to shine all day,
Leaves coming on the trees,
Gentle swaying in the breeze,
Walking our dogs,
Jumping over logs,
I could walk all day,
In the month of May.

Kimberley Harding (13)
Great Torrington Community School, Torrington

I Wish

I wish I might … I wish I may,
I wish you were born on an April day,
I wish I may … I wish I might,
I wish this world to be a beautiful sight.

I wish that I … I wish that you,
I wish everything was blue,
I wish that you… I wish that I,
I wish that we could live in the sky.

I wish that they … I wish that we,
I wish that we could live in the sea,
I wish that we … I wish that they,
I wish that storms went away.

I wish that you … I wish that we,
I wish we could be friends for eternity,
I wish that we … I wish that you,
I wish that wishes did come true.

Jade Courtney (13)
Great Torrington Community School, Torrington

War!

Women cry
Men sob
Children don't even know
It affects us in so many ways
What do I speak of?
War!

Rory Robinson (11)
Great Torrington Community School, Torrington

Good Vibrations

One of the happiest days of my life,
Was going to a festival.

At night you could hear a band playing a
Song in the distance.
The wind was making the tent dance
And wriggle to the beat of the music.

In the morning, there is hardly any people on the site,
The rubbish bins are overflowing with empty beer cans
And plastic cups and plates.

That night you go and see a great band in 4 inches of mud,
As you jump up and down in joy, the mud splashes onto
The next person's leg.

That morning, I peel all the day mud off my leg,
I cry as we leave.

Brendan Vaughan (11)
Great Torrington Community School, Torrington

The Weather

The weather is blue,
The weather is white,
The weather is one beautiful sight.

The weather is stormy,
It's thunder and lightning,
Help me Mum,
This is so frightening.

Mum and Dad,
You're there for me,
You're the one,
That makes me happy.

Sean Borland (12)
Great Torrington Community School, Torrington

15 Nil

The crowd are cheering,
I'm near the goal.
I have a shot,
I've just scored.
The whistle blows,
Final score 15 to me,
Nil to the garden fence.

Adam Stevens (11)
Great Torrington Community School, Torrington

Poverty

Have you listened to rain
On an old tin roof,
As it drips to the floor,
Poverty's proof?
Have you slept on the street,
With the broken glasses
And seen the ruin?
Fortune passes!
Have you been in the lines of
Downcast faces
Who have no jobs?
Poverty embraces!
Have you been the hand behind the gun,
As a storekeeper falls,
Poor and on the run?
Have you cried as your child cries,
From hunger,
Or stopped to wonder?
Why? Poverty's thunder. While the rain slowly drips
To the floor
There at poverty's door,
While we are sitting on the floor,
Watching TV,
Happy as can be.

Charlotte Handley (13)
Grenville College, Bideford

My Room In The Boarding House

My room in the boarding house is a battlefield.
You can find apples, pears, penguins,
Crisps, ham and jam and whatever else you can think of.
My room stinks like a hundred socks.
Not very funny, I know.
Every morning chaos arrives.
Trousers, shoes, socks and all kinds of
Clothes fly around our room.
It's at five-past seven when I wake up and
Run and run downstairs to be on time.
You can hear the water drops on the windows,
The pipes and also the toilets …
That makes me wake up at three in the morning,
Not very funny, I know.

José Felix Velasco (12)
Grenville College, Bideford

The Old Lady

Her face is a shrivelled prune,
Surrounded by grey fading hair,
With eyes as dark as deep wells.

Rocking backwards and forwards on a creaky chair,
Her body bent like a crooked walking stick,
A droopy, unsmiling mouth.

She is a tortoise shuffling around the bare house,
Loneliness and sadness fills her heart,
Dust and cobwebs grow old with her.

The atmosphere feels like a dark, cloudy day,
The doorbell rings and breaks the immense silence,
She creaks across the floor and opens the door.

Warmth and sunshine enter the musty room,
The light dances on her lips
And the warmth of her smile greets her grandchildren.

Rebekah Locke (12)
Grenville College, Bideford

My Dad

He has grey hair like a rainy day
And a moustache like an overgrown bush.

He swims like a stone,
He collects cars as if they were treasures.

His nose is as red as a drunken sailor's,
He thinks he is only thirty-five when he is …

His eyes are as blue as the sea,
His voice is as loud as a howler monkey's.

He has teeth as white as snow and
His feet are as big as an elephant's.

His job is as boring as watching grass grow and
His hands are stained all the colours of a picture.

Jonathan Brookes (12)
Grenville College, Bideford

The Baby

She sits in her cot,
Glaring around,
Just like a tiger ready to pounce on its prey.

Something moves,
She stares around,
A big ugly monster coming towards her.

She grabs her rattle ready to hit.

'Oww!' someone shouts.
She climbs out of her cot, this cage will not hold her,
Planning her escape.

She crawls and crawls,
But the big scary monster gets her
And puts her in her highchair, a more challenging cage,
'She is an annoying as a monkey,' the big monster says.

Baby plans her next escape route,
'Come here Sis, come here,'
Ha ha she has fallen for my trick.

'Oww! Mum she bit me!'
Off goes baby as she escapes out of her highchair
And crawls and crawls and crawls.

Lydia Singer (12)
Grenville College, Bideford

Injustice

They tell me the world is an unjust place,
I already know I've got scars and mud on my face.
Life's not fair!
Because nobody does care,
Life's not fair.

Why is the world so full of injustice?
No one to hug, no one to kiss.
Life's not fair!
Because nobody does care,
Life's not fair!

I wish I had somebody to hold me tight,
Keep me safe all through the night.
Life's not fair!
Because nobody does care,
Life's not fair.

My home like a baked bean tin,
Corrugated iron everywhere,
Like a garbage bin.
Life's not fair!
Because nobody does care,
Life's not fair.

I have my family that is all,
Into the darkness for help I call.
Life's not fair!
Because nobody does care,
Life's not fair.

Holly Rampling (13)
Grenville College, Bideford

The Bin Man

He climbs out of the stinky and dirty truck.
Only 7 am.
The bin man is tired, his eyes droopy like a
Basset hound.
He is smelly from yesterday's job.

Pushed out of the truck like an unwanted dog,
Collecting rubbish from door to door.

Not his day today that's for sure!

Rotting banana skins, apple cores and
Chocolate wrappers strewn around.
'I've had it!' the bin man cries and he stands
Tall and proud like the highest mountain.
Off he goes for another day.

Chloe MacGillivray (12)
Grenville College, Bideford

Bullying

Bullies are not very nice,
They take the mick, even if you have lice.
They think they're cool, they gang up on you,
All about nothing, it's never true.

Sometimes they shout and call you names,
They think it's funny, their stupid games.
They hit, they kick, they think it's fun,
But that's not it, they're not quite done.

Carrying on more and more,
Like a painful bang against a door.
Teachers say they'll give up, leave you alone,
A week later you've left home.

Jenny Eveleigh (13)
Grenville College, Bideford

The Man Next-Door

The man next-door is old and pale,
He's hard, brittle and very frail.

His back is bent like a rusty spoon,
He falls asleep just past noon.

He walks past like a snail,
This is even slower than the mail.

His wrinkles go deeper than a valley,
He says it's because he worked in the gallery.

His hair is like grass in a desert,
He said it came out and it hurt.

The man next-door is old and pale,
He's hard, brittle and very frail.

Tom Marsden (12)
Grenville College, Bideford

The Guard Of Buckingham Palace

He stands there, stiff as stone,
With a black cat on his head.
Without a grudge, without a moan
And a coat of royal red.

When the time has come
And it's the changing of the guard.
He may just cease from being numb
And change his still facade.

His face is red as a ripe tomato,
His sweat a swimming pool.
He stands there like a goalpost,
Unmoving like a ghoul.

His eyes are droopy, grey and solemn,
His nose is red and bent.
Standing straight as a Greek stone column,
Life seems to have been spent.

Sarah Wickes (12)
Grenville College, Bideford

My Grandad

My grandad's as tall as a kangaroo,
His hair's as white as snow,
His laugh is like a hyena
And his ears are like Dumbo's.

His eyes are as bulgy as a tiger,
Who is hunting down his prey,
He's as old as the world,
Which is very old indeed.

He's a waltzing encyclopaedia
As clever as a monkey,
He drives a big car
And crashes into anything he sees.

So this is my grandad,
Boring indeed,
But he's very loveable
And cares about me!

James Guilfoyle (13)
Grenville College, Bideford

Ali QT

Ali QT has arms that are as short as a gremlins,
When he laughs he laughs like a hyena in the tropical rainforests.

He stares at me with his big blue eyes that are as blue as the sky,
His skin is white and pink and is as rough as coral.

His head droops forward like a bent tree on the coast
As he walks to his next lesson, but
His long legs stretch out like a stretch limo when he runs.

Dan Rogerson (12)
Grenville College, Bideford

It's Not Fair!

'You're not going out like that,'
Is what they say,
'What an awful kind of hat,'
It's just not fair.

'Where are you going?'
Is what they say,
'What will you be doing?'
What's it to them?

'You're not going out with them,'
Is what they say,
'They're a load of riff-raff,'
But what do I care?

'Have you done your homework yet?'
Is what they say,
'Take a coat or you'll get wet,'
It's just not fair.

Emma Corrick (13)
Grenville College, Bideford

A Silent Tear

He sits alone with his head in his hands,
Crouched alone in the corner of the street.
Why is he there? He does not understand,
He feels so empty, his life incomplete.

A silent tear trickles down his pallid cheek,
Seeing happy families laugh and smile.
Ravenous and frozen, no food in a week.
His friends disowned him, he wasn't worthwhile.

Prison doors clamp the front of shop windows,
The once bustling streets are left deserted.
Street lamps cast imaginative shadows
Around the bins he has just skirted.

The smiling sun awakes from his rest
And his eyes are filled with rays of light.
Wafts of warm breakfast and fresh morning zest,
Awaken his senses to fill him with spite.

He ponders over the months that have passed.
Regretting wrong decisions he made.
His life is challenging, cruel and harsh,
But more honest than that he chose to evade.

Ashleigh Clayton (13)
Grenville College, Bideford

Just Unfair

There was a wizened old man,
Who sat in a tatty old chair,
Waving a battered old fan,
Thinking that life was unfair.

With an air of despair,
He tears out his hair
And with a stare and a glare,
He thought life was unfair.

His money has all disappeared
And the cat had sat on his hat,
This was not as bad as he had feared,
As the dog had scared the cat.

Whilst eating a pear,
He tripped over the chair
And with a stare and a glare,
He thought life was unfair.

He met a young girl called Jill,
At last there was no more despair,
Jill ran off with a man called Bill,
Why is life so unfair?

He sat in his chair on an éclair.
With a stare and a glare,
He thought, life is so unfair!

Sam Petty (13)
Grenville College, Bideford

Dan Rogerson

Once there was a boy called Daniel
He had green fish-like eyes,
A face not like a spaniel
But like a fish looking for flies.

Dan's quite scary sometimes,
Especially when he can smell chocolates,
He'll do anything to get one,
He'll even do some mimes.

Dan's always eating,
He won't take a beating.
He has fin-like legs,
Ears like pegs
And sharp shark-like teeth.

Dan's always funny,
He'll probably eat a bunny,
He's got freckly white skin
And senses like a pin.

Alastair Quinton-Tulloch (12)
Grenville College, Bideford

The Tramp

He sits in the corner,
Where the cold sharp rain hits him.
The morning sun rises
And the light blinds him with fear.
The rags on his body are soaking wet,
His wet wrinkled face is dripping with water.
His eyes full of fear.
His cold bare feet are shivering wildly,
His shrivelled hands are shaking.
His begging hat is full of old coppers,
His trousers held up by a piece of cord,
His bed is a blanket,
He can only afford one meal a day.

George Snell (13)
Grenville College, Bideford

Bullied

Every day
They always come.
They always get me.
I try to run.
They catch me,
I hide, they find me.
Their evil, grinning faces,
Look down on me,
They beat me up, steal my money.
What can I do? Where can I go?
The teachers don't listen,
The headmaster doesn't care,
My parents are busy,
My sister's always doing her hair.
What can I do?
Where can I go?

Tom Young (13)
Grenville College, Bideford

Poverty

The boy walks through the street
Tattered clothes cover his frail
Little body.
Grime covers his skin
He is going home.

He is greeted by the stench
Of decay
The sight of poverty
And the feel of nothing.

He eats a dinner of cold leftovers,
While thinking about his day,
Working non-stop in the factory.

The boy walks through the street,
Tattered clothes cover his frail
Little body.
Grime covers his skin
He is going back to the factory.

Victoria Charles (13)
Grenville College, Bideford

It's Really Not Fair!

It's really not fair,
When Mum says tidy my room.
It's really not fair,
When Dad says give the dog a groom.

It's really not fair,
When homework has to be done.
It's really not fair,
When people call me dumb.

It's really not fair,
When the rain starts to fall.
It's really not fair,
When people call me small.

It's really not fair,
When I see people in pain.
It's really not fair,
When I get the blame!

Christie Woodley (13)
Grenville College, Bideford

Tramps

You can only find tramps in a stinky place
Because all they do is beg,
You chuck a couple of quid so they can buy some food.

You sometimes see them playing a song
On a one stringed guitar,
Sometimes outside a bar.

You've got to watch out for those stinky tramps,
Or you'll get robbed and feel like them old *tramps!*

Joshua Braddick (13)
Grenville College, Bideford

Concert

We're waiting to see our favourite band
Stamping our feet and clapping our hands.
Here I am sat in the second row
The show's starting soon, I can feel it, I know.

The atmosphere's electric, pulsing through the air
It's twitching up my fingers and shooting down my hair.
Suddenly the lights are off, it takes me by surprise
I can hear a frightened gasp and many startled cries.

A flashing light comes from the stage, I see a silhouette
Of people I know all about, but I've never met.
There's screaming all around me, that I don't seem to hear
A sudden crashing chord rings out straight into my ears.

As they thrash on their guitars I stand and shout and sway
I think to myself silently, *that'll be me some day.*

Elizabeth Tobin (12)
Hele's School, Plymouth

Cheetah

I have a mane until 3 months old,
But even then I don't go bald,
I can be timid and shy,
For that I don't know why.

As I grow my spots will appear,
My coat will get smooth and sheer
My legs are long and sleek,
But my speed I'll always keep.

For the rest I'm fast and slick,
Very cute and very quick,
But if you get on the wrong side of me,
I'll eat you slowly for my tea.

Katy Sheldon (13)
Hele's School, Plymouth

My Clone

I sit all alone,
With nothing to do,
Nothing beside me but a clone.

The clone is my shadow
Big and black,
Waiting to say,
Please come back.

I walk out into the lane
And there it is,
Waiting for me
Calling come play with me.

If not you will be
All alone
Just like me.

So please come back to me.

Jessica McGlinchey (12)
Hele's School, Plymouth

Christmas

Christmas time is the best time of year,
The time where there is nothing to fear,
Snowflakes falling from up high,
Where Santa rides up in the sky.
Presents lying under the tree,
Christmas dinner waiting for me,
Rudolph and Prancer, brilliant friends,
Playing together the fun never ends.
But after the fun has gone away,
Always remember this special day!

Shaun Curtis (12)
Hele's School, Plymouth

Trip To The Shop

I went to the shop to buy some pop,
With a skip and a hop I got to the bus stop.
On the bus I smelt a very strange musk,
As a perfume-splashed woman had entered the bus.
Though today I felt sorrowed,
For the money I borrowed,
Since the can became hollowed
As I paid.
I felt quite numb
Since the liquid was gone
And I owed all that to my mum.

Luke Ambrose (12)
Hele's School, Plymouth

Fish

Pretty fish in the sea,
Blowing bubbles as you can see.
Swimming around in the sea,
Eating all the plankton that they can see.

Kathryn Higgins (12)
Hele's School, Plymouth

Where's My Birthday Gone?

Today is my birthday
but not a present in sight
it seems a dull day
it gives me a fright.

Not a toy or a card
not even a cake
no smell of a pie
ready to bake.

Now I'm at school
my friends act normal today
but I am no fool
they've forgotten my birthday.

As I stumble home
feeling down
I let out a little moan
'cause I'm not wearing a crown.

My birthday is a wreck
I feel so sad
it's not what I expect
I feel so bad.

Keesha Carter-McDonald (12)
Hele's School, Plymouth

Fireworks

Fireworks go boom
On a cold winter's night
Echoing in your room
While you watch the bright light

In the dull winter's night
I had a big fright
As a very big rocket
Hit the street light

Crackle, crackle, crackle,
The glass hit the ground
Leaving sparklers all around.

Danielle Barnes (13)
Hele's School, Plymouth

Children Play!

Up on the hills and far away
There is a place where children play,
They play all day and all night,
They stay there till morning's bright.

Here they come and here they go,
See them running in the snow!

Jade Ellery (12)
Hele's School, Plymouth

Untitled

The warm breeze, people sit out,
Bitter wind makes people wrap up,
People stay up late in summer,
During winter people sleep earlier,
In the summer, hot barbecues sizzle as burgers are put on them,
In the winter people eat chocolates and roast marshmallows
on the fire.

Douglas Miller (13)
Hele's School, Plymouth

Which One Are You?

New is old
And old is new
Which one are you?

Tall is small
And small is tall
Which one are you?

Rich is poor
And poor is rich
Which one are you?

Good is bad
And bad is good
Which one are you?

White is black
And black is white
Which one are you?

If you're old or new, small or tall,
Poor or rich, good or bad
And black or white
God will always love you.

Adam Stead (12)
Hele's School, Plymouth

Candle Love

The candle is the biggest part
Of the love that's in my heart.
It glows a glow of warmth inside,
As calming as a robin's glide.

Love is what makes the world spin round,
It never actually makes a sound.
We all have some love in our hearts,
It's worth more than a billion, a priceless art.

Abigail Jones (12)
Hele's School, Plymouth

Sheep!

Upon the hills there was a flock of sheep,
Who stood still in a massive big heap,
They had bright yellow eyes, a warbling wail
And a kink at the end of their white fluffy tails.
They stood still on the long green grass,
As they watched the cars go speeding past,
They laid there peacefully from morning to night
And rose when the morning was bright.

Laura Shepherd (12)
Hele's School, Plymouth

Television

Television can be good
Television can be bad
Sometimes about food
Sometimes sad.

Television can amaze
Television can bore
Sometimes about people's ways
Sometimes about war.

Television can excite
Television can annoy
Sometimes about a vicious fight
Sometimes about Troy.

Television is a complex place
So many channels
So little taste!

James Watson (12)
Hele's School, Plymouth

Autumn's End

The leaves have been rustled,
The trees are like skeletons,
With twisted bones and branches
Hanging in the air.

Nothing's moving through the trees,
In an eternal sleep,
Woods get dark, street lamps beam
And winter . . . begins.

Lewis Kitte (12)
Hele's School, Plymouth

A Winter's Day

A winter's day,
Cool and crisp,
Glistening candles in the church
And snow falling from the sky,
Blanketing the ground,
Trees swaying in the wind
While people are being forgiven for their sins.

James Lee (12)
Hele's School, Plymouth

As Sad As . . .

I'm as sad as a red lollipop
With no one to lick it.
As sad as a postage stamp
With no one to stick it.
As sad as an apple
With no one to pick it.

As sad as a ball
With no one to catch it.
As sad as a stable
With no one to latch it.
As sad as a twin
With no one to match it.

As sad as a fire
With no one to light it.
As sad as an orange
With no one to bite it.
Sad as a person
With no one to love them.

Holly Wilson (12)
Lipson Community College, Plymouth

As Lovely As . . .

As lovely as a beach with no tide out
As lovely as a wedding with a beautiful bride in
As lovely as a friend who stands by your side.

As lovely as a diamond with someone to wear it
As lovely as a secret with someone to share it
As lovely as a baby with no one to dare it.

As lovely as a lollipop with no one to lick it
As lovely as a sticker with someone to stick it
As lovely as a clock to watch it tick-tock.

As lovely as a person with no one to fight it
As lovely as a peach with no one to bite it
As lovely as a teacher being polite to it.

Lucy White (12)
Lipson Community College, Plymouth

But You're As . . .

You're as nice as a butterfly
Flying out to freedom.
You're as tall as a basketball player
But prefer medium.

You're as beautiful as a princess
With the diamante crown on your gentle head.
You're as golden as an angel
Always dreaming the truth on your bed.

You're as cute as a bunny
Hopping around all day.
You're as artistic as Picasso
Entering every competition in May.

But you're as lonely as a song without music
With no sound or beat like a broken heart.
You're tearful like the pouring rain
Whose lake has been thrown away in a wooden cart.

Siobhan Tracey (12)
Lipson Community College, Plymouth

The War

In the silence of the night where the moon glows a hazy white
everything is peaceful,
then the monsters come out to play.
Earth-shattering noises loom upon the once so peaceful land, closely
behind these monsters are men marching in time with each other.
100
90
80
70
Now it begins!
The first crack of a bullet is created
and then another and another,
each soldier's head pounding as the unbreakable noise gets worse
and worse.
Screams, shouts and pleas for help echo as each man falls
like a leaf falling from a tree.
The unbreakable noise is nothing compared to the
monstrous tanks when they make their mark.
Boom!
There is only a couple of seconds to think as the next
murderous shell is loaded,
and then once again
boom!
The ground beneath shakes back and forth like a tennis ball
at Wimbledon.
More hours go by and more men join, hoping for the
bloodshed to end soon,
but this is only the beginning!

Josh Steels (12)
Lipson Community College, Plymouth

Sad

I am as sad as a letter with no one to post it.
As sad as a party with no one to host it.
As sad as a talent with no one to boast it.

As sad as a ball with no one to bounce it.
As sad as good news with no one to announce it.
As sad as a winner with no one to trace it.

As sad as a trophy with no one to win it.
As sad as a cafe with no one to sit in it.
As sad as a rubbish bag with no one to bin it.

As sad as a puppy with no one to stroke it.
As sad as a feeling with no one to evoke it.
As sad as a bond when somebody broke it.

Jessica Patrick (12)
Lipson Community College, Plymouth

I'm As Silly As . . .

I'm as silly as a monkey not liking a banana.
I'm as silly as Ella not listening to Nirvana.
I'm as silly as my mum liking modern music.
I'm as silly as a dog trying to groove it.
I'm as silly as a mouse chasing a cat.
I'm silly and that is that.

Chanelle Newcombe (12)
Lipson Community College, Plymouth

I'm As Random As . . .

I'm as random as a Goth being best friends with a chav.
I'm as random as a monkey eating up a crab.
I'm as random as a bakery selling kebabs.

I'm as mad as a chav not speaking like a janner.
I'm as mad as the Queen head banging to Nirvana.
I'm as random as a 2 year old acting like my nanna.

I'm as nerdy as a chav without its Lacoste.
I'm as nerdy as a push-over acting like they're cross.
I'm as nerdy as a baby acting like the boss.

Ella Kenny (12)
Lipson Community College, Plymouth

I'm As Happy As . . .

I'm as happy as the sun with someone to shine on.
As happy as a hippo for someone to splash on.
As happy as a plum with someone to be my chum.

As happy as a firework with someone to light it.
As happy as a strawberry with someone to bite it.
As happy as a bright day with the sun to lighten it.

As happy as an octopus with two more legs.
As happy as a kitten with someone to care for it.
As happy as a promise with someone to keep it.

Stacey Hancock (12)
Lipson Community College, Plymouth

You're As Lonely As . . .

You're as lonely as a prisoner in solitary confinement.
You're as lonely as a small child lost in a crowd.

You're as lonely as a song without its music.
You're as lonely as the sun without its shine.

You're as lonely as a lover without their love.
You're as lonely as me without my friends.

Hannah Baugh (12)
Lipson Community College, Plymouth

Crazy Things

I can be . . .
an artist, acrobat or a barmy baboon
a crazy car driver, a dirty dancer
an eventful elephant or a frantic, funky farmer
a groaning giraffe or a happy hen
an interfering iguana or a jeering jockey
a keen kangaroo or a laughing looney
a moaning maid or a naive, naughty newsagent
an outstretched orang-utan or a pretty predator
a quibbling queen or a typical toddler
an unusual UFO or a vicious viper
a witty weatherman or an interesting xylophonist
a yelling yachtsman or a zany zebra.

Lewis Barnes (12)
Lipson Community College, Plymouth

My Dad

If he was an element, he would be Earth.
If he was in darkness, he would be light.
If it was morning then he would be fright.
If he was money, he'd be a million pounds.
If he were an animal, he'd be a mountain bear.
If he was extinct he'd come alive again.
If it was winter he'd be an ice rink.
If he was a colour, he'd be a bright shade of orange.
If he wasn't a mountain bear he'd be a whale.
He would like to be a chimpanzee or a human.
If he could fly, he wouldn't.
If he couldn't fly, he would.
He would be nothing like a dead rat drying in the heat of the sun
Shooting unwound blue strings out of a circle-shaped mouth.
He would be a big gorilla dancing in the light of the sun
Or a fat, strong wolf howling.
He is shiny and bold like the brisk sun on a summer afternoon in Asia.
He is my dad, the Santa of the family.

Zachary Leon (13)
Liskeard School, Liskeard

Let Me Be Your Friend In Great Difficulty Or Need

Let me be your friend in need
Breathing in your air
Let me be your war indeed
Because I truly care

Let me be your squadron leader
Being your handsome hero
Let me be your garden weeder
Turning your weeds to zero

Let me be your paramedic
Sorting our your pain
Let me be your headache
That's driving you insane.

Tim Sloman (15)
Plymouth Hospital School, Plymouth

Untitled

Inside I'm screaming
Outside I'm dreaming
Of what life could be
Hopefully one day, I will break free

It's like I can't breathe
When you're inside of me
I know these voices in my head are mine alone
And none unsaid

People say it's serious
But inside I'm curious
I feel like I'm not me
This person inside I don't want to be.

Kirsty Griffin (13)
Plymouth Hospital School, Plymouth

In The Shadows

Haunting, daunting world of woe,
Suddenly you become my foe.
Eyes glazed over, nothing behind,
Eclipsing the thoughts of my mind.

Aspirations, world of hope
Finding I can no longer cope.
Tears start falling down my cheek,
All at once I'm frail and weak.

Each perfect rose has its thorn,
The perfect life starts at dawn.
Life's become a convolution,
I'm still waiting for a revolution.

Naomi Jones (17)
Plymouth Hospital School, Plymouth

The Un-Named

My confusion is your illusion
Leading me astray
How could something deep inside me
Refuse to go away?

Wrestling with the thoughts you feed me
Not knowing whether to agree
Insanity the new normality
I've lost sense of all reality.

Searching for an absolution
Reaching any resolution
Pondering the image I want to be
Holding on, waiting to be free.

Aimee Clark (15)
Plymouth Hospital School, Plymouth

Gingerbread Man

Ginger, Ginger, in the oven with his big sherbet button
And his black eyes twinkling like spies.

He makes a dash for the door, but tripped over the floor.
He will trip over no more as he is out to scream and shout
He was trotting down the road
Thinking of a code
When a crowd howled, 'Yummy after it.'
So Gingy hit the top of it
He found a fox, near a box
Looking across a lake with a tasty bake
Right at his feet, he couldn't resist to eat.
I will take you across like a boss
As long as you hop on my nose
So I can handle you like a hose
Now we are here, let me gobble you like beer
And up in the air he was
But down in the throat he went
What a good treat, I did eat.

Ashley Wonnacott (11)
St James' School, Exeter

Cinderella

There was a little girl, who had a glass pearl.
Her mother died and her father survived.
Not long after, there was a big disaster.
Cinderella had a stepmother, who was always under cover.
And her ugly stepsisters, whose feet were full of blisters.
Made Cinders life a world of strife.
Along came a letter, making Cinders feel better.
An invite to a ball, for one and for all.
To stop Cinderella going, the chores kept flowing.
A fairy godmother came to call
And said, 'Cinderella, you'll go to the ball.
So forget about this mess, let's sort out a fancy dress!
I've sorted out transport, all right?
Just make sure you're back by midnight.'
She was the talk of the town in her long flowing gown.
As she danced with the prince, the stepsisters winced.
They knew they were history, the rest . . . is another story.

Amber Goff (11)
St James' School, Exeter

Jack And The Red Kidney Bean

Jack noticed one day
A gorgeous girl was out to play.
So he went straight up and asked her out
She said, 'Of course, I'm not doin' nowt!
I only eat the red kidney bean
The bigger the better
I like them mean!'
So Jack went to the market that day
And heard a mucky man say,
'Come buy these kidney beans
Eating them will mean
Your date will love you for evermore
But use them wisely as there isn't a cure!'
So Jack had the lot
And cooked them up,
He made the mix big
He made the mix mean!
And that day gorgeous came around
She heard the sound of the beans
Sizzling in the frying pan!
She said, 'Is it safe to eat
As it looks awfully sweet?
I'll try it though, you wait and see
I'm sure it will make me smile with glee.'
She tried the mix
She said, 'Good grief!'
As she smiled with disbelief.
'I love it!
Most of all I love you
But just one second, I need the loo!'

Laura Tippett (12)
St James' School, Exeter

Cinderella

There once stood a girl with eyes like a jewel
She had a stepmother who was a fool
She adored the outdoors
However her sisters and stepmother thought she had no cause
Her name was Cinderella
Her stepmother said she could have done so much better
She had to obey her stepmother
She longed for someone special, a devoted lover
She worked all day, poor Cinderella was forced to stay
She was so upset, Cinderella had no one, not even a pet.
Her sisters only cared for their looks
However Cinderella was more interested in fascinating books.
One day Cinderella's stepsisters went to a ball
Expecting to find their prince handsome and tall.
Just after her stepsisters left, Cinderella saw an amazing sight
It was an astonishing sight, there stood Cinderella's fairy godmother.
Now Cinderella was ready to find her love
Prepare to shine and glisten like the stars above.
The fairy godmother placed her spell
And now Cinderella had a chance to find her love.
Cinderella arrived at the ball and her radiance shone across the room
No longer was she surrounded by doom
Cinderella saw her prince, her destiny was clear
She was overcome with fear
It was a joyous occasion when she left the night had passed
She knew the happiness was to last.

Charlotte Abdoviszadeh (12)
St James' School, Exeter

Little Red Riding Hood

Little Red Riding Hood, went into the wood,
Wearing her suit with a little red hood,
Along came a tiger, who sat down beside her,
And he said, 'Hello, my name is Fred.'

Then the wolf with a terrible grin, strolled up with a look of pure sin,
'Hello my dears,' he said to them,
Smiling he said, 'I'm just a gem.'
'Yeah right,' said the tiger, with a lot of anger.
'Where are you going?' the wolf asked Miss Hood.
'Only to see Grandma who lives in the wood.'
Some time later the wolf had got to the house,
The house that had not a mouse,
The wolf ate Grandma whole, like a lump of coal.
He put on her dressing gown and let out a frown.
Little Red Riding Hood came in with curiosity and said,
'I know you're in disguise, I'm very wise.'
'Oh very well, I'm going to eat you now.'
'No you're not,' came a familiar voice,
'I'm going to eat you! You don't have a choice.'
Out popped Grandma who fainted with fright
OK, that's all for now, night-night.

Luke Batchelor (11)
St James' School, Exeter

Little Red Riding Hood

One day in the gloomy wood, the big scary wolfie stood.
He and his grinning teeth hid beneath
The branches of the dark, dark trees,
Where were all the butterflies and bees?
He watched Red Riding Hood skipping past,
Then he put on his fake leg cast,
Wolfie hunched along, yelping out,
'Ouch, ouch, this hurts without a doubt!'
'Oh you poor, poor wolf,' Red Riding Hood cried.
The wolf let out a scream and sighed.
Poor wolf, he was left all alone,
While Riding Hood walked to Grandma's home.
He crept along just like a mouse.
Grandma answered the ringing door,
Her eyesight was very poor.
'Hello, hello, you may come in,
Unless you're trying to sell something!'
Grandma got eaten up in one big gulp,
It was like the wolf was the Incredible Hulk.
The naughty wolf crept into Grandma's clothes,
He gave Red Riding Hood a rose.
The wolf tried to eat Red Riding Hood,
But back away from him she stood!
She hit him hard with a great big stick,
It made him dizzy and feel quite sick!
Red Riding Hood then ran away,
That was the end of the wolf, *hooray!*

Abby Thomas (11)
St James' School, Exeter

Jack And The Beanstalk R3 Mix

There was a boy called Jack, who had a dumb mother who was slack,
she wasn't very bright at all, her face was the size of a football.
They lived on a country farm, where foxes caused chickens harm.
On that farm there was a cow called Daisy, who was greedy and lazy.
'She's rotten,' Jack's mother said,
'She sleeps on our gorgeous bed and does her business down the
stairs, she's fat and eats our apples and pears.'
So Jack and Daisy went to the dodgy market
and sold Daisy for three beans and a carpet.
His mum was furious and had a frown
so she jumped off Debenham's in town.
Poor Jack's beans were very rare,
so he was cautious and gave them care.
He watched the beans grow and grow
until they were bigger than the nose on Pinocchio.
Jack was strong and climbed the bean
and up there in the clouds he'd seen
a big, huge giant, who was a client.
For jack was big and bold,
he shot the giant and stole his gold.
Jack jumped down the beanstalk, what a laugh,
he was smelly and took a bath.
Now Jack was rich and had a good trend.

Ben Burton (11)
St James' School, Exeter

Goldilocks And The Three Bears

Once upon a time there lived three little bears,
Waiting for their porridge they sat on their chairs,
But when it was served Daddy said, 'This porridge is too hot!'
Mummy bear said, 'It would be, it just came out of the pot!
So Daddy bear, Mummy bear and Baby bear went down town.
Now Goldilocks had a chance,
She climbed through a window and fell down!
She saw the porridge, she was amazed, it made her gaze and gaze.
Finally she thought she'd try it
So she tried Daddy bear's, bit by bit.

It was so *hot*, she nearly had a *fit!*
Next she tried Mummy bear's, it was so tasty she sat on a chair.
She was eating but then she found some ice,
She spat it out, she didn't think twice.
She thought she'd try Baby bear's, it looked just right!
'Yum,' she exclaimed, it was so tasty
She thought she'd be there all night!
She then saw some comfy chairs, which were made out of *rabbit hairs!*
First she tried Daddy bear's one, which was very scarred,
It was also too hard!
Goldilocks thought Mummy bear's would be better,
So she picked up the letter, it was dusty, she thought it was from the
loft, she moaned, 'God, it's way too soft.'
Baby bear's was her last chance, so she took a glance.
So she sat right down, this time it didn't make her frown!
She was feeling tired so she moved on to the beds
Daddy bear's was horrible so was Mummy bear's,
Their beds were like lead.
But Baby bear's was so soft she fell asleep.
Meanwhile the bears came back with a sheep,
They found Goldilocks in Baby bear's bed
Baby bear got a sword from the shed and chopped off her head
A few days later was her funeral . . .

Farihah Choudhury (11)
St James' School, Exeter

War At The Door

The smell of smoke,
So bad it made me choke.
The sound of bombs,
They were even louder than the sound of gongs.

The amount of people I heard had died,
It was so upsetting people cried.
The sounds of the guns blazed,
The number of people that were getting grazed.

People died and people fell,
For the people that were injured it was hell.
There was lots of blood on the floor
The colour was as red as the Earth's core.

People lay there a ghostly white,
It really was a ghastly sight.
There were loads of heads rolling,
It was like a game of bowling.

Tanks were shooting,
People puking.
Some of the floor was brown because it was mud
But most of it was covered in blood.

Ashley Hobbs (14)
St James' School, Exeter

Jack And The Beanstalk

Jack's mum told him to go to the market
He took his car, but couldn't park it.
And then he took out his cow, Daisy
But saw a man who was crazy.
He offered Jack some magic beans
So Jack slotted them in his jeans.
He ambled home for his dinner
Where his mum was looking thinner.
'Jack, what is it you've brought back?'
And she threw out the small sack.
'Those beans cost you Daisy
I can't believe you're so lazy'
And off to bed poor Jack went
Thinking about the time he spent.
In the morning a sight he saw
A huge beanstalk out of the floor.
He climbed it before his mum was up
And took a drink in a cup.
Up and up, little Jack went
And soon he came to a vent.
It took him to a castle of a man
Whose hands were the size of a van.
A golden goose Jack did see
And thought, *that's for me.*
He went back soon after
This time he saw a lamp of gold
And wanted to keep it for when he was old.
He was chased by the giant, after his feast
But chopped down the beanstalk and killed the beast.

Adam Rose (11)
St James' School, Exeter

Goldilocks

Goldilocks went to the house of the three bears,
She looked around
There were beds, porridge and chairs.
Goldilocks foraged, for some porridge.
It was too hot, it was too cold,
Baby bear's was fine
And no mould!
She sat down in a chair,
Too hard was that chair
And she cried,
'That's not fair!'
The other too soft
Then Goldi coughed,
She sat down and thought of fame.
Then she broke the chair,
Who will she blame?
She went upstairs for a nap,
In came the bears,
Including Baby bear with his cap!
'Someone has eaten my meal,'
Called Baby bear making a big deal.
'They've even broken my chair,'
But Father bear did not care.
Baby bear said,
'There's someone sleeping in my bed.'
Father bear scared her
That was no joke!
And off she ran
With a can of Coke.

Chelsea Lee (11)
St James' School, Exeter

The Rise And Fall Of Jack And The Beanstalk

Jack had a cow called Daisy, who was extremely lazy,
Jack and his mum must be crazy, they wanted rid of poor Daisy.
Jack went to the market square where people sell things, common
and rare,

Jack walked past a man, selling a bear,
As it shouted, 'Stop brushing my hair.'

As Jack didn't want to sell the poor cow,
Out of the blue Jack yelled, 'Wow!
For now he knew how, to sell his cow.

Then up came some girls, whose hair was nothing but curls,
They were all wearing pearls,
Jack impressed, said, 'Give us some twirls.'

One girl said, 'Selling the cow?'
'Yes,' whispered Jack, but forgot how,
Silly Jack thinking wow, one girl said, 'Do you want to sell it now?'

Said a girl in her teens, 'Take these three magic beans.'
Jack thought, *could this mean will it all end in happy scenes?*

The bean started to grow, reaching the sky,
Jack at the bottom wondered how high?
Jack climbed up shouting, 'My oh my!
Look at that giant eating that pie.'

Jack picked up the golden goose,
Made his escape fast and loose,
The giant chased Jack, looked like a moose,
Jack cut the beanstalk, the giant was juice.

Emma Jewell (11)
St James' School, Exeter

Three Billy Goats

There was once three billy goats,
Who had lovely, thick, woolly cots,
They trotted and plotted across the land,
Until they saw an ugly green hand,
It belonged to a troll, who loved to rock and roll.
The troll sat underneath his bridge
And waited for meat to put in his fridge.
The baby goat tried to cross,
But the troll thought he was boss.
'I'll get my brother on you,'
Cried baby goat as he hit the troll with his shoe.
The bigger goat came to fight,
But the troll was too much of a sight,
'I'll get my brother to bite,'
Screamed the bigger goat with quite a fright.
So on came the big boy looking very, very coy,
He beat the troll, like he had no soul,
He bit, scratched and kicked,
As time tocked and ticked.
The troll fell into a well,
And all of the goats crossed the bridge,
And emptied out the old troll's fridge.
Inside they found the frozen bodies of their mates,
Destined for the troll's dinner plates.
The goats wouldn't melt, until the sun shone full pelt.
Then the goats started to play
And they managed to have a nice day!

Ellen-Mary Haydon Wright (11)
St James' School, Exeter

Little Red Riding Hood

Once upon a time, there was a big chime.
There was a little girl, her necklace was made of pearl.
The girl's name was Little Red Riding Hood,
She was strolling through the wood
With a basket of fruit, she had a red suit.
There was a big wolf, who was playing some golf.
He spotted Red Riding Hood, strolling through the wood.
He stopped his game, for was very sane.
He'd had an idea, after having a can of beer.
He sprinted to old Grandma's house and ate a mouse.
He got to old Grandma before Red Riding Hood could say bran.
She stopped to pick some berries
And found some nice, juicy cherries.
She stopped to talk and then carried on to walk.
She got to Gran's home, and took out a comb.
She opened the door and walked on the floor.
'My, Grandma, what a big mouth you have!'
'All the better to eat you with chav.'
The woodcutter stood on some poo
And chopped the wolf in two.

Matthew Knight (11)
St James' School, Exeter

The Killers Of War

Guns were blazing
People fell
For those who shot them
It was Hell.

People lay there
Pale and white
It really was
A horrific sight.

Arms were scattered
All over the place
Blood was dripping
From every face.

Men choking
From their blood
Eyes popping out
As they lay in the mud.

Matthew Channon (14)
St James' School, Exeter

Snow White

Once upon a time, in a land where the sun shone
Snow White lived with her dad who was loving and kind
Her dad went dating to find a new wife
Because his old one had been killed by a very sharp knife.
The stepmum was jealous of Snow White's good looks
So she made potions and read millions of beauty books.
The stepmum wished Snow White could be dead
But Snow White went on holiday to France instead.
Whilst visiting many countries she hitch-hiked around
She partied with seven little men, not far from the ground.
The dwarves took her back to tidy their home
With a little small garden including a gnome.
All seven dwarves loved Snow White quite dearly
Even Grumpy liked her - well - nearly!
Deep down in the mine the dwarves worked daily
Snow White cooked tea singing with the birds gaily.
Discovering Snow White was still alive
The stepmum vowed to see her Monday at five.
Happily the dwarves went off to their work
Whilst the stepmum began to sneakily lurk.
Towards Snow White she went in her flowing cloak
She held out an apple, so Snow White could choke.
Snow White was polite so couldn't refuse
The stepmum was pleased because she wouldn't lose.
Snow White fell into a sudden deep sleep
Worried dwarves found her there in a heap.
She lay asleep for years and years
Miserable dwarves shed loads of tears.
A prince came by and kissed her soft lips
Saying, 'Wake up Snow White, please cook me some chips!'

Bethan Ashelford (11)
St James' School, Exeter

War

As I hear the guns bang, one, two, three
The stench of dead flesh crept up on me
Pools of blood all around
And bodies cover most of the ground.
Men scream, some even cry
Before long I see 'em die.
I close my eyes and count to ten
But when I open them it all starts again
My hair is full of dirt and mud
And my clothes are soaked in blood.

Kirsty Dare (14)
St James' School, Exeter

Little Red Riding Hood

Little Red Riding Hood, went into the wood
There she met a dinosaur, who raced her to Grandma's door.
The dinosaur won and had a fight
And Grandma won and said, 'Don't come back, alright!'
Little Red Riding Hood gave Grandma the dinner
And said, 'Grandma, you're such a winner.
I can't believe you got the dinosaur in the eye with a fly.
How did you do that, because he was so fat?'
'Oh because I'm just great and that is that.'
So they both went off and had lunch
And ate grapes that were in a bunch.
Sandwiches, chocolate and yoghurts to eat,
Oh what a fantastic, delightful treat.
'Time to go my Little Red Riding Hood.'
'Why Grandma, can't we stay in the wood?'
'Otherwise you'll be late for your mum
And she will get angry and smack my bum.'
So off they skipped, hand in hand
And along the way saw a brass band.
'Oh Grandma, let's stay to hear them play.'
'No Red Riding Hood, we haven't got all day
Mum is waiting outside my house,
Hope we get back before she sees the mouse.'
Safely back, just in time
For there was the mouse beneath the sign.
'Don't just stand there, get a mallet
Try and put it near the pallet.'
'Time to go now, Mum is here,
Please don't cry, just say goodbye.'

Simone Marillier (11)
St James' School, Exeter

Little Red Riding Hood

There was a girl who dressed in red
And always listened to what her mother said.
She had to go to her Grandma's door
As part of her weekend chore.
She wanted something to eat
So went to the butchers for some meat.
Now she arrived at the end of the wood
And there she saw something, stood
It was large, brown and had big eyes
And looked as if he told bad lies.
He looked the poor girl up and down
And changed his smile into a frown.
He finally spoke with a low deep tone
And reached into his pocket, he found a bone
It made the girl give a shriek
And made her nerves go all weak.
He started to worry and made a quick run
She couldn't have any more fun.
When she found the right house
She saw a small creature, it was a mouse.
'Hello,' said Red Riding Hood
But then she saw something and I thought I should
It was a piece of clothing her grandma wore
But it was hard to notice a store
Of bones and flesh, she let out a shout
But her mouth was covered by a doubt
She found out it was a surprise
And it was wise
To know the wolf was a whole joke
To know and make sure the small girl was definitely awoke!

Ummaymah Qureshi (11)
St James' School, Exeter

Jack And The Beanstalk

Jack and his mother were very poor,
They had to sell Daisy the cow.
One day they had a knock on the door,
It was Mrs How, she was the tax lady,
They had to sell Daisy for money,
Oh dear, old Daisy, it wasn't very funny.
Jack sold Daisy for five magic beans,
When Jack came home his mum was cross,
She sent him to bed without any dinner. But under the moss,
There was a mirror and he was sure he was getting thinner,
There was a sprout poking up,
Jack went to bed and then it got bigger,
Jack found his cup,
He was sure it had a picture of Tigger,
He went and had a cup of tea,
Then he had a shower,
Then he ate chips and peas,
Jack went out and picked his mum some flowers,
Jack looked up at the stalk,
It must have been as high as the sky,
Then Jack saw a stalk,
Jack's mum looked like she was going to cry,
Jack climbed up to the very top
Where he went into the giant's castle,
Jack climbed down with the giant's golden mop,
Then cut the stalk and the giant fell down with a parcel!

Sarah Wakeley (11)
St James' School, Exeter

The Three Bears

Once there were three bears that grew a lot of hairs.
There was one big, one medium and one small,
He loved to play in the hall.
They woke up one morning and heard Big Bear snoring.
Mother bear made some porridge,
In their house in Norwich.
It was far too hot, so they left it in a pot.
They went out, not knowing Goldilocks was about.
She went in, and walked into a bin.
She smelt the nice porridge, in the house in Norwich.
She liked it a lot, and stared at the empty pot.
She tried the two big chairs, they were covered in hairs.
She sat on the little one, it broke and gave her a sore bum.
She went into the next room and fell over a broom.
She went in the big bed, the pillow was too big for her head.
The next bed was the same too, and didn't hear the coo-coo.
She fell asleep in Baby Bear's bed
She woke up to see a bear's head.

Estelle Hacq (11)
St James' School, Exeter

The Three Little Pigs

One sunny day
Little pig sat in hay,
His mother in their cottage
Sorting out a blockage
Which was making her stressy
And she got very messy.
(Now that you are all grown,
It's time for you to buy a home.)

Little pig says, 'I'm making my house out of brick,'
Middle pig says, 'I think I'm going to be sick.'
Seeing the brown soggy blockage
Down in the little white cottage;
Big pig says, 'I'm building mine from straw
Because I'm quite poor.'
'So am I,' says middle pig, 'but I'm building mine with sticks
Because I cannot afford to buy bricks.'

Mother pig started to cry
When she said her last goodbye.
Soon their houses were complete
They all lived in one big street.
Mother pig visited little pig's house of bricks,
Middle pig's house of sticks
And big pig's house of straw.
Mother pigs says, 'Oh, I am proud of you all!'

Michaela Ward (11)
St James' School, Exeter

Red Riding Hood

Red Riding Hood set out one day,
To her godfather's place: old and grey.
Her uncle Joe, he had some gas,
So he waited for his niece to pass.
When Red Riding Hood strolled along the path,
She yelled, 'Uncle Joe! You need a bath!'
'Never mind that, just pull my finger!'
'No, no! I'd rather linger!'
Uncle Joe, he sprinted fast
So Red Riding Hood would get there last.
Uncle Joe, crept in quite sneaky,
Dressed as the Godfather, really quite freaky!
Red Riding Hood knew there was something wrong,
But she couldn't put her finger on it, so she carried along.
She went in - still quite cautious,
Saw the Godfather, very nauseous!
'Your Uncle Joe,' he did cry,
'He's eaten far too much lamb pie!
He couldn't wait to cut the cheese,
It smelled so bad, I couldn't breathe!'
She went on in, holding her nose
And saw Uncle Joe, in the Godfather's clothes.
'cut it out, I know it's you!
And I don't want to pull that finger, too!
Anyway, I have 'pine fresh scent',
To wipe away your dent!'
'No!' he cried,
'Just eat slower,' so he tried.
So they all lived happily ever after,
With absolutely no toilet laughter!

Alex Seabrook (12)
St James' School, Exeter

Jack And The Beanstalk

Once there was a boy called Jack
Who had a cow that wasn't fat.
Jack's mum told him to go to the market,
'But why?' Jack replied.
'It's always eating the carpet.'
His mum just lied.
Jack and the cow went to the market but no one would buy it.
Why don't I just take her home and fry it,
But then someone said,
'I'll take that cow instead of it dead.'
He offered three beans.
Jack placed them in his jeans.
He went home feeling proud,
But found out his mum had frowned.
She threw them out the window
Then she cackled, 'Ha ha bingo!'
But overnight they grew,
A beanstalk came into Jack's room and it looked like he flew.
On the beanstalk he went up and up,
Then he thought, *I can't jump.*
In a big house lived a giant,
Jack thought it was Myan.
Then the giant said, 'Fee fi fo fum I smell an Englishman.
He's trying to steal my goose, where's my gun?'
Jack took the golden goose.
The giant's trousers went loose.
There was a loud crash, then no one ever had a frown.

Mashud Rahman (11)
St James' School, Exeter

All About Me

My name is Sammy
I like to play with my friends.
I live with my mum and our cats
And my sister who drives me round the bend.
I like to play on my skates and go to the park,
We like being outside but have to be in before dark.
I like my new high school but I have to work very hard.
Some people have been bullied
So I have to be on my guard.

Sammy Cooper (11)
St Luke's Science and Sports College, Exeter

The Tiger

The tiger, the tiger mates with the lion to make the liger,
They come in all sizes,
Some big some small,
But most of them fascinate all.
Because of the poachers a lot are killed,
Just like shark fins are grilled.
But those who survive,
Are now more alive
The tiger, the tiger.

Daniel Kendall (11)
St Luke's Science and Sports College, Exeter

Cancer

There were three of us and we're still together *just!*
After all we've been through and to think we could lose her just
like that.

Cancer wrecks everyone's life.
So don't make a joke.

No one knows what it is like until you get it.
But she is strong and we all stick together whatever happens.
She had it before and we thought it had gone but now we just
feel as bad

All we can do is give blood and hope.
But that won't make it better
I wish it was gone!

So don't laugh. Don't joke,
Because cancer wrecks everyone's life
Not just the person that has it.

Hannah Aplin
St Luke's Science and Sports College, Exeter

Hallowe'en

Hallowe'en comes round again
Everybody's worried and scared.
The day it arrives all the children are out,
Scaring the elderly and giving them a fright.

By the time it is dark all the big kids are out,
With their top masks, scary costumes
And all their might.

Hallowe'en is a cold dark night
And nobody likes it . . . tonight!

Emily Hiscox (11)
St Luke's Science and Sports College, Exeter

All About Me

I am a sweet perfume
A kitten: soft and cuddly
As noisy as children playing
I am as shiny as the sunshine
An orange: healthy and nice
I am the bright sun.

Emma Rowett (11)
St Luke's Science and Sports College, Exeter

The Truth

What are we?
Scruffy blighters, crims,
They think we're dossers
And winos, but really,
They don't know the truth.

To them we are invisible
To them we are down-and-outs,
But they don't know who we are,
They don't know why we are like this.
They don't know the truth.

Maybe this is a disease,
Or maybe it's our fault,
Nobody knows
And nobody cares.
They don't know the truth.

If they only cared enough,
To ask, to find,
If only they gave,
As much as they could.
Maybe, they would know the truth.

Maybe they would help,
To get us on our feet again,
Then we could thank them,
For helping, for caring.
Then they would know the truth.

Kirsty Dean (13)
St Luke's Science and Sports College, Exeter

Homelessness

Sitting here, alone tonight
With the world whizzing by
Rejected from a society
That has no time nor care

Sleeping rough, the whole year through
Depending on strangers
And living on their contributions
Unsure of what will come

And I'm not the only one
There are thousands homeless
All with a different story to tell
All, with the same ending.

Zöe Rio (14)
St Luke's Science and Sports College, Exeter

Homelessness

H ell on Earth being homeless
O ver is my previous life
M um oh how I miss her
E vil people make me sleepless
L et no one attack you with a knife
E very night my dreams are a blur
S ending messages to my family
S eeing their faces smiling calmly
N ever eating enough to live
E ven now I hate my father
S leeping rough is a waste of life
S ighting people to give me money.

Christopher Morris (13)
St Luke's Science and Sports College, Exeter

My Poem

Rugby on a pitch, rugby in a ditch.
Rugby on the floor, rugby is a chore.
Rugby at half time, rugby at bath time.
Rugby keeps you fit, just a little bit.
Rugby is fun, especially in the sun.
Rugby can be bad, if you get really mad.
Rugby in the morning, can be really boring.
Rugby late at night, can give you a fright.
Rugby in the summer, can be a bit of a bummer.
But rugby in the day is fun hip hip hooray.

Dominic MacNamara (14)
St Luke's Science and Sports College, Exeter

Homeless People On The Streets

Homeless people on the streets
Only wanting somewhere to sleep
Only to get some food and drink
Only to get some money
Only wanting somewhere to sleep
Only to get some sweets
If only I had some money to buy a house
If I had something to keep me warm
And it would not be cold.

Melissa Sampson (13)
St Luke's Science and Sports College, Exeter

Where Shall I Go?

Living on the streets, nowhere to go
All I need is food and drink
Somewhere to keep me warm
All the way through the night
Without getting moved on by the cops

I have no friends and family who care
What shall I do? Where do I go?
Back home, no I can't
They'll kick me out again
I never did anything wrong they just don't love me

I spent all day begging
I only got £1.50
How am I supposed to live on that?
Only had a sandwich for my tea
Got no money left now
What am I going to do?

Am I going to live to the next day?
Will anyone miss me?
I always wanted to make a change to the world
Which I'll guess I'll never do.

Jade Willingham (13)
St Luke's Science and Sports College, Exeter

Winter Nights!

The coldest nights,
Come round again.
The soft snow falls
On the grey snowy roads.

Children playing tennis,
With balls of snow.
All of the kids dripping wet,
From the fight!

The coldest nights come round again!

Katie Omand (11)
St Luke's Science and Sports College, Exeter

Happy Hallowe'en!

Temptation is rising,
It's a dark, dark night.
Hallowe'en is here,
Be prepared for a fright.
The witches are out,
Back from the dead,
It's nine o'clock,
We should be in bed.
But not tonight,
Not on Hallowe'en,
Cos the witches are here
And I'm ready to *scream!*

Steffanie Herd (11)
St Luke's Science and Sports College, Exeter

Homelessness

Night after night disappointment.
Night after night alone.
Day after day, no encouragement.
Why did they take that tone?

Night after night dangers.
Night after night left out.
Day after day more strangers.
Always being moved on.

Night after night more pleading.
Night after night so ill.
Day after day no feeding.
The days and nights and so still.

Charlotte Childs (14)
St Luke's Science and Sports College, Exeter

Sleeping Rough

A different doorway every night
Every night a different fright
Getting peed on by a drunk
Or getting beaten by a punk

A different doorway every night
Every night a different fright
Getting bruises on my back
And owning nothing except a pack

A different doorway every night
Every night a different fright
Sleeping on a floor of stone
And every night you're all alone

A different doorway every night
Every night a different fright
From your family you're the only one
And you know that they're all having fun

A different doorway every night
Every night a different fright
You lay awake while time passes slowly
And then you think if only, if only.

Ellie Sketchley (13)
St Luke's Science and Sports College, Exeter

Homelessness

You see them everywhere begging for cash,
but many people try to ignore them.
They act as if they have somewhere to dash,
or they say they are awaiting a call.

They own nothing but the clothes on their backs,
few lucky ones own a sleeping bag too.
There are many of them, stack upon stack
and there's a lot normal people can do.

It is an increasing problem for us
and we have to find a way to stop it.
It seems that no one cares or makes a fuss
all the homeless wish they could just quit.

Not one single person gives them the time,
all of this misery should be a crime.

Sally Foss (13)
St Luke's Science and Sports College, Exeter

The Homeless Poem

Every night,
When it is dark
I'm on the streets,
All day long.
With nothing to eat
Or drink
And very little money
Which I spent
When it's either
Rain or shine
I'm always cold
When I sleep
I'm freezing
Sleeping
On people's doorways
Always chucking me out
When they return
Very rude
Throwing me out
What am I
Supposed to do
Sleeping rough
Every single night
Or if there is
Any hope
Someone will come
And save me
From living on the streets
To a nice warm home to go to.

Christopher Rand (13)
St Luke's Science and Sports College, Exeter

Homeless

H ard stone floor, no comfy bed
O pen doorways do they crave
M atted hair, no brush to use
E ndless begging for spare change
L onging for someone to show they care
E veryone giving dirty looks
S leeping rough is so bad
S leeping rough is so sad.

Max Bennett (13)
St Luke's Science and Sports College, Exeter

Homeless

H ome I wish I could see
O n my own no one to plea
M y life is Hell, if only you can see
E vil may or does haunt me
L ife is the only thing keeping me going
E vil has been growing
S omeone out there, I don't know who
S omeone out there, I need you
N ever I thought my prayers would be answered
E vil has been lifted it has left me
S omeone has finally found me
S omeone I hope will take care of me.

Matthew Ayton (14)
St Luke's Science and Sports College, Exeter

What's It Like To Be Homeless

H omelessness is horrible
O bviously nobody wants me
M ost people ignore me
E veryone walks past talking, but not to me
L ife just cannot get any worse
E scape was the only way out
S orrow is the only way forward
S cared all night long
N o one to comfort me, no one to care
E ven dogs live better than me
S tuff being thrown on top of you
S leepless nights.

Becky Lee (13)
St Luke's Science and Sports College, Exeter

Homeless

H omeless people living on the streets
O nly wanting somewhere to sleep
M ost nights freezing cold
E vil shadows do they face
L ingering in the dark as you pace
E very night so dark and cold
S leeping in the doorway, nowhere else to go
S hivering with the cold and with hunger.

Sasha Lovell (13)
St Luke's Science and Sports College, Exeter

Homelessness

H omeless people everywhere
O n the streets of London
M en and women both of a kind
E veryone walks right past
L onely with no one to look to
E verywhere they sleep is uncomfortable
S un rises and they get up to beg
S leep is bad, so you're tired the next day
N owhere to stay, got to keep moving
E veryone keeps away from them
S ad how this happens
S ad it happens today.

Sam Woodman (13)
St Luke's Science and Sports College, Exeter

Christmas Eve

On Christmas Eve
It's a silent night
All warm and tight.
All of a sudden
I hear a bump,
I wake up scared in a fright.
I run downstairs,
I see Father Christmas,
I think I'm in a dream . . .
He goes back up the chimney
Never to know what I've seen.

Rachel Sharratt (11)
St Luke's Science and Sports College, Exeter

Hallowe'en

Hallowe'en, Hallowe'en, Hallowe'en,
Everything's spooky and mean.
Hallowe'en, Hallowe'en, Hallowe'en,
Everyone's trick or treating.
All the sweets we collect we sit at home eating.
Hallowe'en, Hallowe'en, Hallowe'en,
Graveyards are empty, the spirits rise,
Witches on broomsticks, what a surprise.
Hallowe'en, Hallowe'en, Hallowe'en,
Ghost haunting houses,
Scaring all the mouses (mice)
Hallowe'en, Hallowe'en, Hallowe'en,
Frankenstein ugly and mean,
All of them ever so mean,
How I love
Hallowe'en!

Bethany Meredith, Emily Ford & Megan Hobbs (11)
St Luke's Science and Sports College, Exeter

Why Me Teacher?

The teacher, he bullies and beats me, I know not why
I haven't told anyone, I dare not try
I hide every pain-filled mark
So my parents are left in the dark

He haunts me in my dreams at night
Showing me that it will never be alright
Is it because I'm weak, because I'm poor?
All I know is that I can't stand it anymore

The teacher, he bullies and beats me
When is there going to be a night when I don't cry?

Faye Windsor (11)
St Luke's Science and Sports College, Exeter

Twilight Hour

In the famous twilight hour,
Darkness shows its evil glower.
It is a time of fear and dread,
Raise the power of the dead.

Children run, shout and scream,
People avoid this awful scene.
It is like a piece of Hell,
It only stops at the dawn bell.

This is the evil of the twilight hour.

The evil grows with every second,
Devils laugh and shall be beckoned.
The depths of Hell shall rise,
it shall be the world's demise.

This is the evil of the twilight hour.

Rieuan Elliott (11)
St Luke's Science and Sports College, Exeter

At Home (A Poem About Domestic Violence)

The anaemic beach sighs and moans,
her feeble cries are blatantly ignored.
Expanses of beach are smeared with spume,
spewed from the sea's raging jaws.
The ashen shore awaits the incoming tide,
advancing at an evil,
leisurely pace. For he knows
that her frozen tidal wave of rock is no match for him,
and his raving tidal swings.
Battered branches protrude from the sand,
sallow, salt-stained eyes glower at the slumbering ocean
which softly kisses her feet in repentance;
for the rusty metal scars, still visible on her front.
The stony face is bruised, from long hidden hurts,
like a rotten layer cake.
Her confident horizons evaporate into the mists,
like blood, smudged on a cheek.
Gulls, the permanents patrollers of the coast,
cry to themselves as events unfold below,
but are drawn away by the call of the wind
to search for silvery treasures of their own.
Strings of Welsh candles flash and flicker,
mockingly, in her direction,
for she is fixed in a nook of the land,
trapped by her opposing companion.
The solitary daffodils inside the woods
comprise the only surviving,
fragment of her beauty.

Hannah Bolt (14)
St Margaret's School, Exeter

Bitten By A Fool

The night has fallen, an eerie night,
In the air hangs the scent of fear and fright,
As I leave the cosy caress of the crypt
For my number one victim whom I've so often nipped.

With the eye-splitting brightness of sunlight away,
There is no element of danger as there is in the day.
So I can travel swiftly across the dark night skies;
Knowing only my victims will encounter surprise.

I see a window open wide,
So I take a peek and dive inside.
A youthful maiden lies within,
With blood-red hair and pale white skin.

Dinner tonight will be such a rare treat,
This beautiful maiden will have good 'gore' to eat.
I put my fangs to her beautiful neck;
And puncture two holes . . . in the wrong place!
Oh heck!

Emily Sheen (13)
Torquay Grammar School for Girls, Torquay

Christmas!

The days leading up to Christmas,
are exciting for us all,
the weather becomes colder
and snow begins to fall.

Christmas trees appear in windows,
decorations all around,
at the night of Christmas Eve,
you cannot hear a sound.

From the moment that you wake up,
it's presents galore!
Lots of gifts for everyone,
for you there's even more!

There's a Christmas meal at midday,
all festive and jolly,
crackers by each plate,
mistletoe and holly.

Crackers are pulled one by one
and the meal will then start,
turkey then Christmas pudding,
sharing love from the heart.

Remember to enjoy Christmas,
for it comes only once a year,
it's always a special time,
a time for Christmas cheer!

Jen Huntington (12)
Torquay Grammar School for Girls, Torquay

To Catch A Falling Star

Sometimes I wish I could catch falling stars
And keep them like shining dreams and wishes

Destined to fade as the light catches them
But to hold onto them for that moment of triumph
Overwhelms you and makes you soar.

You feel unbeatable . . . unstoppable
'Til the stars die
Along with all the emotions invested into them,

Like capsules of longing
All the things you most desire to be and have
Shining in your hands;

But to lock up all aspirations
Is not a happy ending . . .

Let all your wishes soar free
And fate will guide them
They will find their path
If you just let them soar

I still often wish
I could catch a falling star
And then I remember all the wishes I have,
All the things I possess
Are already there in front of me.

If you have love
You have caught your falling star.

Millie Hawkins (12)
Torquay Grammar School for Girls, Torquay

The Rose

A mass of blood-red petals that swirl around each other,
Petals soft as velvet,
So delicate and beautiful,
It looks good enough to eat

Standing gracefully on an emerald stem
The rose wants attention,
It draws you towards it,
The rose stretches out to welcome you

It tempts you with all its beautiful colours and its sweet smell,
It drags you round and round through the petals
Until, you reach its jet-black heart.

Alice James (12)
Torquay Grammar School for Girls, Torquay

Lost Love

Empty heart,
being torn apart.
Hurting inside,
the rules to abide.

Soul disappeared,
hatefulness appeared.
Love missing,
no more kissing.

Parents fighting,
anger biting.
The fear of a slap,
the sounding of a thunder clap.

Caroline Hickey (11)
Torquay Grammar School for Girls, Torquay

Alone

Sitting by the door
Hoping and waiting for
Someone to love and to care,
But instead, dreaming they are there.

Cold long nights go by
Without even a hi
So small and alone
Not even noticed in her home.

A dirty look here and there
Why is it so unfair?
Again she feels all alone
Being treated like a dog and bone.

The only time he realises her
Is when he has a fist to share
She shows no mercy, no plea
Just the look, 'Why don't you love me?'

Day after day, night after night
Until he brings on the next one-man fight
Bruised and battered,
Her confidence shattered.

Sitting by the door
Hoping and waiting for
Someone to love and to care,
But instead dreaming they are there.

Amy Carruthers (12)
Torquay Grammar School for Girls, Torquay

Neglect

Stroked and cuddled,
Loved by all,
Fed and protected,
Then came a downfall.

Beaten and mocked,
Traumatised and scared,
No one to love it,
No one to care.

Huddled away,
In a corner bleak,
Cowering from light,
Tears start to leak.

No one to hear it,
No one at all,
Shaking and shivering,
Curled up in a ball.

No one to go to,
As it weeps,
Happy dreams slip away,
In its last sleep.

Sprawled on the floor,
A body weak and thin,
Can we forgive
This mighty sin?

All alone, neglected and sad,
Lifeless, limp and dead,
Never again to see the light of day,
In its eternal bed.

Emma Beard (11)
Torquay Grammar School for Girls, Torquay

The Palace

The palace standing high
See every bird fly in the sky.
People have lovely dreams
Whilst peacocks scream.

Red curtains so bright
Chandeliers for lights
Ceiling glow
Outside it snows.

Shaped like a wedding cake
People always celebrate.
Set out on a green tablecloth
Up high there are flies and moths.

Carpets so clean
That they gleam.
Rushing around
My feet not touching the ground.

People awake, people asleep
People dreaming about their feet
Adults drive in their cars
Whilst children play with metal bars

Whilst people are drinking
Children are thinking.
As the palace closes
The doorman poses.

The palace standing high
See every bird fly in the sky.
People have lovely dreams
Whilst peacocks scream.

Molly Blackler (11)
Torquay Grammar School for Girls, Torquay

Scared

Scared to death
Don't take a breath
He slams the door
And throws the coat to the floor

Don't feel loved
I get pushed and shoved
He makes me feel
I'm no big deal

My heart beats fast
How long will the fear last?
He hits me hard
I could run a yard.

Fleur Goldman (11)
Torquay Grammar School for Girls, Torquay

The Mind

I don't care

I do what I want
I live free
And that's all I'll be

I don't care
Some think I'm evil
Some think not
But my father thinks I'm a spot

I don't care
I'm a murderer
I find it interesting
But hey who cannot

I don't care
I move from one to one
Being friendly then dumping
I don't listen, only to my recent friend

I don't care
I don't do what I'm told, never
Listen to me if you wish
But go away if you won't

I don't care
I do what I want
I live free
And that's all I'll be.

Alison Doble (11)
Torquay Grammar School for Girls, Torquay

The Tulip Touch Girl

(Inspired by 'The Tulip Touch' by Anne Fine)

I met a new girl yesterday,
I asked her over to come and play.
Her hair was wavy, long and fair,
She looked quite dirty, but I didn't care.

Her name was Tulip, I loved it so
I never wanted her to go.
She smiled at me and I smiled back,
We went outside so I grabbed my mac.

We played together happily,
We screamed and shouted together with glee.
Her rosy cheeks and flowing hair,
I couldn't help but stop and stare.

A pretty bird flew down close by.
It was so elegant I couldn't lie,
But Tulip screamed at the tiny bird
And something quite terrible I heard.

The sound was terrifying, the thud and a squawk.
She had killed the bird and then began to talk,
'It was annoying anyway!'
Then suddenly she ran away.

Now after seeing what she has done,
It has ruined all our fun.
The bird was innocent, it had done nothing wrong.
But now it is dead and has lost its song.

Jordyn Read (11)
Torquay Grammar School for Girls, Torquay

The Tulip Touch - The Palace

(Inspired by 'The Tulip Touch' by Anne Fine)

Step into the palace, it's warm and bright,
Windows sparkle in the glistening summer light.
You'd love looking at the palace at the first light of dawn,
And to somersault forever down the clover-studded lawn.

Don't try and count the bedrooms 'cause you'll never reach the end,
It's the perfect place for hide-and-seeking with a friend.
The cherry-red sofas you could bounce on all day long,
Or to skip down the corridors whistling a happy song.

At December in the palace it's all scarlet and gold,
The decorated trees are beautiful and bold.
All along the terraces coloured lanterns brightly wink.
The lights on the trees go blink, blink, blink.

All around are people as happy as can be,
Either lying on the lawn or sitting by a tree.
It doesn't matter if it's raining or the skies are blue,
The palace is the place to be to see your dreams come true!

Florence Cowling (11)
Torquay Grammar School for Girls, Torquay

Natalie And Tulip

(Inspired by 'The Tulip Touch' by Anne Fine)

Bawling-brother
Terrible-mother
Attic-counter
Urn-mounter
Kitten-chaser
Step-pacer
Animal-kisser
Friend-misser
Tortoise-smacker
Shell-cracker
Big-worrier
Quick-scurrier
Path-follower
Loud-hollower
Cat-harmer
Dad's a-farmer
Game-player
Sofa-layer
Kettle-boiler
Fun-spoiler
Parents-older
Coat-holder.

Gemma Collins (11)
Torquay Grammar School for Girls, Torquay

Who Is Tulip?

(Inspired by 'The Tulip Touch' by Anne Fine)

Days of dumbness,
Roads of bones,
They're the games that make Dad groan.

Happy families,
Tickle the baby,
They're the games that hurt Tulip maybe?

Natalie's very confused,
She doesn't know just what to say,
Tulip's her friend but she's fading away.

Tulip's parents are really scary,
Just like the forgiving smile.
Playing with Tulip makes it all worthwhile.

Their friendship is rocky,
While Tulip lies,
Natalie just wants to cry.

A murderer of animals?
Animals' lives she may nick,
Who is Tulip?

Olivia Bishop (11)
Torquay Grammar School for Girls, Torquay

The Palace

(Inspired by 'The Tulip Touch' by Anne Fine)

Glittering sign,
Sudden shriek,
Darting peacocks
All the week.

Revolving doors,
Shiny floors,
Marble stairs,
Collapsing lairs.

Open lounge,
Vast green lawns,
Beautiful flowers,
Working long hours.

Look out to the fields,
Beauty unreal,
There she stands,
Kitten in hand.

Things will change,
How will we comprehend?

Rebekah Woolnough (12)
Torquay Grammar School for Girls, Torquay

The Lone Liar

(Inspired by 'The Tulip Touch' by Anne Fine)

Look at them, watching me
What is it that they see?
Why won't they ask me to play?
Why tell me to go away?

Don't they know their looks hurt?
Why treat me like some dirt?
Why won't they ask me to play?
Why tell me to go away?

I don't like to tell lies,
But I'm bad in their eyes.
Why won't they ask me to play?
Why tell me to go away?

I'm not loved, but they are,
I'm shoved, left in the dark.
Why won't they ask me to play
Why tell me to go away?

They'll never see me cry,
No tears will fall from these eyes.
Why won't they ask me to play?
Why tell me to go away?

I met a girl today,
Maybe, sometime, we'll play.
She asked me to come and play,
She never said, go away.

The girl's called Natalie,
Oh, what fun this will be,
She asked me to come and play,
She never said, go away.

Olivia Ross (11)
Torquay Grammar School for Girls, Torquay

The Peacock's Cry

(Inspired by 'The Tulip Touch' by Anne Fine)

Under the blazing sun,
Tulip tells lies by the tonne,
Screech, screech the peacock's cry,
Telling everyone Tulip's nearby.

Overhanging trees,
Shelter clover-studded lawns from the breeze,
Corridors made to be skipped down,
Endless fun to be found.

Under the blazing sun,
Tulip tells lies by the tonne,
Screech, screech the peacock's cry,
Telling everyone Tulip's nearby.

Cellars to explore,
There can't be much more,
But there are still blanket cupboards to be hidden in,
And a sunset to be seen.

Under the blazing sun,
Tulip tells lies by the tonne,
Screech, screech the peacock's cry,
Telling everyone Tulip's nearby.

Bethanie Jones (11)
Torquay Grammar School for Girls, Torquay

Natalie's Visit

(Inspired by 'The Tulip Touch' by Anne Fine)

I won't turn back, I won't go home,
I'm on the doorstep all alone.
I feel so scared my throat is tight,
If Dad found out I'm here tonight
He'd be so cross, without a warning,
No more fun until the morning.

Hearing footsteps coming nearer,
Vision's starting to get clearer.
Hear a bolt, a latch and chain,
Don't think I'll come here again.
The door's unlatched, it's open wide,
I take a breath and step inside.

Down the hall I bravely walk,
Looking round, I don't dare talk.
Dust and grime is everywhere
Mrs Pierce is standing there
With her beg-your-pardon smile,
I hope this visit is worthwhile.

Tulip's room is out of bounds,
Mrs Pierce's whistling sounds,
Tuneless, mad and scary too,
Mr Pierce asks, 'Who are you?'
Tulip's just a shell at home,
Just a girl that's all alone.

Now I think that it is time
To leave this shocking world behind.
Go back home and don't come back,
I think this family all do lack
The courage needed to take care
Of their daughter, standing there.

Molly Williams (11)
Torquay Grammar School for Girls, Torquay

The Palace

(Inspired by 'The Tulip Touch' by Anne Fine)

Peacocks pace,
filled with grace,
sweeping drive,
feels alive?
Antique doors,
polished floors.
It fills me with such unease.

Cherry-red chairs,
swooping stairs,
cherubs gold,
carpet rolled,
every room,
seems to bloom.
It fills me with such awe.

Emma Rowbottom (11)
Torquay Grammar School for Girls, Torquay

That Girl!

(Inspired by 'The Tulip Touch' by Anne Fine)

That girl!
She's gonna pay,
She wrecks what we do and she wrecks what we play.

That girl!
She gunged my paints,
She ripped up my coat and made Natalie faint!

That girl!
She's such a fool,
She stepped on my mice when I brought them to school!

That girl!
It brings a tear,
Just the name makes me shiver with fear.

That girl!
She drives me mad,
She bent my bangles and swore at my dad!

That girl!
She's gonna pay,
She wrecks what we do and she wrecks what we play.

Elizabeth Thorpe (11)
Torquay Grammar School for Girls, Torquay

The Big Blue Sea

The big blue sea
Is the sea for me
When the moon is silvery bright.
The big blue sea
Is the sea for me
It comes out every starry night.

The waves rush in
The waves rush out
They go back to their ocean domain.
The goldish sand
The silvery sand
Makes a path, or a road, or a lane.

The waves have changed they are still and calm
As I walk along that sand.
The sun shines bright
A golden light
In a far and distant land.

Holly Wilce (11)
Trinity School, Teignmouth

Snow Lion

The snow lion, guards her kingdom of ice and snow
She gallops through the mystical forest
And preys on the fleeing deer
She sleeps in the echoing caves
And watches over her sleepy cubs like a hawk.

Matthew Coombes (11)
Trinity School, Teignmouth

Who Am I?

I hit the rooftops,
I hammer the windows,
I come from clouds,
Who am I?

I flow down rivers,
I fall down waterfalls,
I come from clouds,
Who am I?

I glide out taps,
I'm in the bath,
I come from clouds,
Who am I?

Have you guessed yet?
Do you know?
Who am I?
I am water!

Sally Elizabeth Bascombe (11)
Trinity School, Teignmouth

The Ocean's Secret

I watch the gentle ocean lapping the sand,
like a big mouth coming to swallow the beach.
The magnificent sea sparkled in the moonlight,
like a recently polished silver-plated dish.
The shoals of fish glided and jumped,
like pieces of foil floating around.
Then I see a fantastic creature,
jumping and diving in and out of the light.
I watch it for hours, just to see,
the flick of the tail of a humpback whale.

Cara Childs (12)
Trinity School, Teignmouth

A Dinosaur Poem

They walked this planet a million years ago,
But they certainly didn't invent the bow!
They could shake the ground with their own weight,
And every night they would stay up late!

Some of them would eat the green stuff,
But I don't think they ever saw a bus!
The others weren't quite as nice,
Because they turned their friends into rice!

A lot of them were as big as a bus,
But unlike a bus they didn't rust!
They just grew and grew and grew,
Until they would make a very large stew!

There was this guy I knew who had large teeth,
But I know for certain that they weren't very weak!
His teeth could crush skin and bone
And he may well have lived in Rome!

So who are these guys that I'm talking about?
Why it's the dinosaurs that are about!
Well what can I say about all of these creatures?
Is that most of them would need a cage in the metres!

Jonathan Hadley (13)
Trinity School, Teignmouth